North Korea's Cyber Operations

Strategy and Responses

AUTHORS

Jenny Jun
Scott LaFoy
Ethan Sohn

PROJECT DIRECTORS

Victor D. Cha
James A. Lewis

A Report of the CSIS Korea Chair

December 2015

ROWMAN &
LITTLEFIELD

Lanham • Boulder • New York • London

About CSIS

For over 50 years, the Center for Strategic and International Studies (CSIS) has worked to develop solutions to the world's greatest policy challenges. Today, CSIS scholars are providing strategic insights and bipartisan policy solutions to help decisionmakers chart a course toward a better world.

CSIS is a nonprofit organization headquartered in Washington, D.C. The Center's 220 full-time staff and large network of affiliated scholars conduct research and analysis and develop policy initiatives that look into the future and anticipate change.

Founded at the height of the Cold War by David M. Abshire and Admiral Arleigh Burke, CSIS was dedicated to finding ways to sustain American prominence and prosperity as a force for good in the world. Since 1962, CSIS has become one of the world's preeminent international institutions focused on defense and security; regional stability; and transnational challenges ranging from energy and climate to global health and economic integration.

Thomas J. Pritzker was named chairman of the CSIS Board of Trustees in November 2015. Former U.S. deputy secretary of defense John J. Hamre has served as the Center's president and chief executive officer since 2000.

CSIS does not take specific policy positions; accordingly, all views expressed herein should be understood to be solely those of the author(s).

ISBN: 978-1-4422-5902-7 (pb); 978-1-4422-5903-4 (eBook)

Center for Strategic & International Studies
1616 Rhode Island Avenue, NW
Washington, DC 20036
202-887-0200 | www.csis.org

Rowman & Littlefield
4501 Forbes Boulevard
Lanham, MD 20706
301-459-3366 | www.rowman.com

Contents

Preface

The impetus for this study was the cyber attack against South Korean banks and media agencies in March 2013. The subsequent cyber attack against Sony Pictures Entertainment in November 2014 made our research efforts directly relevant to the U.S. policy debate on cyber conflicts. The U.S. government's designation of North Korea as the responsible party for the act, which released sensitive files and communications from Sony, was a surprise to many in the cybersecurity field and in the Korea expert community as few had estimated the Democratic People's Republic of Korea (DPRK) to be capable of such activity.

We started to look into the issue and found quickly that there was very little open-source and unclassified information about North Korean cyber operations. There had been occasional studies done by scholars and industry, but the literature was sparse at best. Our initial conversations found the lack of any single go-to source primer about what we know about these North Korean capabilities. This revelation led us to consider a one-year study that would comb the open-source literature, conduct interviews, and perform field research to get a better understanding of North Korean cyber operations.

The research team, consisting of the primary authors on this report, Jenny Jun, Scott LaFoy, and Ethan Sohn, had the right combination of cybersecurity, North Korea, and international security expertise to undertake the work. At CSIS my colleague James Lewis, director and senior fellow in the Strategic Technologies Program, agreed to serve along with me as senior authors and advisers for the project.

The caveat with any study on North Korea is that one does research with very little information. There are no websites that can be easily accessed of North Korean origin; no studies of their cyber strategy; and no experts that one can easily access. North Korea is considered one of the hardest intelligence targets in the world.

Through our concerted efforts, this study offers one of the first primers in English on the strategy behind North Korea's cyber operations; the institutions within the DPRK government that are associated with these operations; and a study of North Korea's technology base. We learned a great deal in completing the study, and learned quickly of its interest to the public and private sector when we released the executive summary for the study in September 2015.

We would like to thank the current and former CSIS Korea Chair staff, including Sang Jun Lee and Ellen Kim, the Strategic Technologies Program office, and the CSIS Publications Office for their tireless work on this project. We hope that you will find the research and analysis in this study useful.

Victor Cha
Senior Adviser and Korea Chair
CSIS

Acknowledgments

The primary authors would like to express deep gratitude for those who made this project possible, through their hard work, patience, and support. This project would never have been possible without Dr. Victor Cha, who encouraged an extended study of the topic, generously agreed to provide institutional support for the project, provided constant guidance throughout numerous revisions and overhaul of the content, and, most importantly, sparked our interest on North Korean issues years ago as a mentor. We also thank Dr. James Lewis for offering his extensive expertise and insight into this topic throughout the project.

We thank and acknowledge the efforts of staff of the CSIS Korea Chair, especially Ellen Kim, Sang Jun Lee, Marie DuMond, Andy Lim, and Lisa Collins, who provided extensive assistance to our project and made sure that all components of the project progressed seamlessly. We would also express deep gratitude to our interviewees, including Joseph Bermudez Jr., Catherine Lotrionte, Lim Jong-in, Kim Heung-kwang, Yoo Dong-yeul, Choi Sang-myung, as well as many others who wish to remain anonymous. They shared their extensive knowledge and insight, which was vital to the creation of this publication. We also thank interns Min-hyung Kang and Min-jeong Lee for their hard work and time dedicated to this project.

Jenny Jun, Scott LaFoy, and Ethan Sohn

Abbreviations

APCERT	Asia Pacific Computer Emergency Response Team
APEC	Asia-Pacific Economic Cooperation
APEC-TEL	APEC Telecommunications and Information Working Group
ASEAN	Association of Southeast Asian Nations
C4ISR	command, control, communications, computers, intelligence, surveillance, and reconnaissance
CBM	confidence building measure
CERT	computer emergency response team
CNE	computer network exploitation
CNO	computer network operations
CSIRT	computer security incident response team
DDoS	distributed denial of service
DMZ	demilitarized zone
DNI	director of national intelligence
DPRK	Democratic People's Republic of Korea (North Korea)
ECCM	electronic counter-countermeasure
EO	executive order
EW	electronic warfare
GPS	global positioning system
GSD	General Staff Department of the Korean People's Army (North Korea)
IP	Internet protocol
ISO/OSI	International Standards Organization/Open Systems Interconnection
IT	information technology
ITU-IMPACT	International Telecommunication Union–International Multilateral Partnership Against Cyber Threats
KCC	Korea Computer Center (North Korea)
KPA	Korean People's Army (North Korea)
KPTC	Korea Posts and Telecommunications Corporation (North Korea)
KWP	Korean Worker's Party (North Korea)
MND	Ministry of National Defense (South Korea)
MPAF	Ministry of People's Armed Forces (North Korea)
MSS	Ministry of State Security (North Korea)
NDC	National Defence Commission (North Korea)
NIS	National Intelligence Service (South Korea)

NKIS	North Korea Intellectuals Solidarity
PIC	Pyongyang Informatics Center (North Korea)
PLA	People's Liberation Army
PLC	programmable logic controller
R&D	research and development
RGB	Reconnaissance General Bureau (North Korea)
ROK	Republic of Korea (South Korea)
SCADA	supervisory control and data acquisition
TCP/IP	transmission control protocol/Internet protocol
TTPs	tactics, techniques, and procedures
UN GGE	United Nations Group of Government Experts
WMD	weapons of mass destruction

Introduction

Purpose, Scope, and Methods

PURPOSE

This report aims to provide a comprehensive overview of North Korea's cyber strategy and operations based on open-source literature. There has been significant media coverage of North Korea's high-profile cyber attacks, but there have been limited attempts to delineate patterns in behavior and understand motivations. Current open-source literature does not adequately answer why North Korea is pursuing cyber capabilities, how they are organizing and executing their operations, and what this means for strategy and policy.

Furthermore, the discussion on North Korea's cyber operations has not yet been contextualized into existing fields of study. The topic lies at the nexus of North Korea studies as well as an emerging literature on cyber warfare, but insights from these bodies of literature has so far not been properly incorporated into the topic and vice versa.

This report mainly aims to provide a top-down perspective on North Korea's cyber operations by identifying patterns, trends, and strategic thought behind its behavior. This report does not aim to be a technical forensic analysis of North Korea's cyber attack tools and methods.

The report seeks to create a base reference document on North Korea's cyber operations for policymakers, scholars, and professionals in multiple fields as well as those who do not necessarily have specialties in North Korean military, cyber, or military strategy. More specifically, this report pulls together knowledge of cyber strategy and North Korean national strategy in an attempt to fully explain what North Korean cyber strategy is. This includes detailing what the defining characteristics of cyberspace are, how cyber capabilities have been used historically, how the organization of the North Korean military and intelligence apparatus has incorporated cyber and related capabilities into their technological bases.

SCOPE

The term *cyber capabilities* is a broad and potentially confusing phrase. For purposes of this report, cyber capabilities specifically refers to a means of accomplishing goals or exerting influence in or through cyberspace. This, very broadly, includes general activities such as hacking, data exfiltration, criminal activity, and espionage. It also includes narrowly defined activities such as computer network exploitation (CNE), computer network defense (CND), and computer network operations (CNO).

This report focuses specifically on cyber capabilities as a means of national action. It does not focus on purely criminal or espionage activities, nor does it focus on non-state actors. It does not deal with issues of attribution in cyberspace. While very important, attribution is a technical problem that is not discussed here. The authors assume that responsible and accurate attribution will be achieved before considering implementation of any recommendations explored in this report.

This report makes a deliberate attempt to avoid overly technical or political phrases that inhibit strategic discussion. Many assessments can get lost in the technical weeds or through too broad political suggestions that lose meaning. This report will focus on how North Korea's cyber capabilities fit into the DPRK national strategy and what that means for the United States.

METHODS

The evidences and conclusions of this report are based on open-source information analysis, encompassing English- and Korean-language media sources. This includes books, academic journals, and government reports, testimonies, and statements; websites and blogs; and expert interviews conducted by the authors across the public, private, and academic sectors in both the United States and South Korea. The methods do not include any independent technical analysis of cyber incidents commonly attributed to North Korea.

A Note on Open-Source Reporting on DPRK

The primary objective of this report is to provide a comprehensive, reliable picture of DPRK's cyber operations drawn from open sources so that information can be shared with a wide range of audiences including policymakers, scholars, and the general public. Nonetheless, the authors fully recognize the limits of reporting on DPRK based on open sources, and outline some of its limitations below as a caveat to readers. They believe that transparency regarding sources, dates, and citations, where possible, is the best policy for allowing readers to draw their own judgments regarding the validity of statements in this report. The authors also encourage others to challenge and augment the research toward a clearer and nuanced understanding of cyber-related issues.

DISINFORMATION

The biggest danger to relying on open-source information when reporting on DPRK is its susceptibility to disinformation, a deliberate dissemination of false or inaccurate information. DPRK military doctrine places emphasis on the importance of denial and deception operations, and the lack of alternative open sources of information due to the closed nature of DPRK's society creates an ideal condition to carefully control what information is released externally. For example, organizations often have pseudonyms to obfuscate their mission and order of battle. For example, the Reconnaissance General Bureau (RGB) has also been reported to be alternatively named as the 586th Army Unit. Disinformation can also be used to both exaggerate a particular capability while downplaying or disguising others. This information can be deliberately disseminated via state media, leakage of false documents, or manipulation of information by utilizing the adversary's collection methods.

ECHO CHAMBER EFFECT

Another problem in researching this issue through open sources is an echo chamber effect in the media that brands unverified statements as established facts over time through repeated reporting by other outlets. This effect is further amplified in the case of DPRK's cyber operations capabilities because so little alternative sources of information are available, hindering cross-referencing or verification. There is also little effort to check whether a piece of information is outdated or not, despite the fact that DPRK's cyber operations are rapidly changing in structure and capacity. Language barriers amplify this effect, where English-language journalists often need to rely on already translated, secondary sources of information from major ROK news outlets. This is a big source of potential misinformation. The authors deliberately searched for alternative interpretations of widely accepted narratives and dispute such narratives when appropriate. Original primary statements and sources were evaluated for reliability and consistency. Information was cross-referenced with independent methods, such as satellite imagery, when possible.

INCENTIVES OF SOURCES TO OVERESTIMATE AND UNDERESTIMATE

Information is not always shared in an impartial manner. Although the content of the information shared may not be false or inaccurate, it is not always free from the biases and ulterior motives of the source sharing the information. Some entities may release overestimated data in the hopes to increase their budget, heighten prestige of their organization, push forward a related political agenda, or escape blame from another issue. Some entities may underestimate in an effort to downplay its threat or escape responsibility. The same applies to individuals. The recently increased policy and media attention to North Korea's cyber operations capabilities may also further fuel these incentives. Where possible, the authors try to provide the full context in which such information was shared, point out any inconsistencies in the source's assessments, and provide alternative assessments from other sources if they are available.

FUTURE CONSIDERATIONS

Open-source research on this issue is further complicated by the existence of several information gaps between communities. First, a language barrier exists between researchers, restricting English-speaking researchers from accessing much of the existing Korean-language research on this issue. Second, researchers from a social science background have a hard time interpreting technical information related to cyber operations, and vice versa.

Third, information sharing between the public sector and the private sector is limited in both the United States and South Korea. An effort to close some or all of these information gaps may considerably advance our understanding of cyber-related issues in the future.

Executive Summary

North Korea is emerging as a significant actor in cyberspace with both its clandestine and military organizations gaining the ability to conduct cyber operations. However, there is no comprehensive standard literature about North Korea's cyber capabilities that takes an integrated view of the topic. Existing research is fragmented in pockets of strategic, technical, and policy pieces, though no individual study reaches far enough to create a standard reference document about North Korea's cyber capabilities. This report aims to fill the void, integrating Korean- and English-language information sources and existing work in each respective field, and creating a foundation for future deeper research.

Cyber attacks in South Korea and the United States have recently been associated with North Korea. The U.S. and Republic of Korea (ROK) governments attribute recent incidents, including the November 2014 attack against Sony Pictures Entertainment and the March 2013 attacks against South Korean banks and media agencies, respectively, to North Korea. These attacks have shown that the country is capable of conducting damaging and disruptive cyber attacks during peacetime. North Korea seems heavily invested in growing and developing its cyber capabilities for both political and military purposes.

These attacks raise important policy questions. Existing research does not comprehensively answer questions about why North Korea conducted these and similar attacks, how it has been able to launch these attacks, and what this implies for U.S. strategy and policy. This report attempts to answer these questions with a top-down view of North Korea's motivations, as well as its government and military organizational structure. It also provides analysis on how these factors affect North Korea's behavior in cyberspace. The authors hope to provide decisionmakers with a better understanding of North Korean patterns of behavior as well as allow them to anticipate and respond to future incidents.

THE STRATEGIC CONTEXT OF DPRK CYBER OPERATIONS

An understanding of North Korea's existing political and military strategy is necessary to assess North Korea's cyber strategy. Historically, North Korea has relied on various asymmetric and irregular means to sidestep the conventional military deadlock on the peninsula while also preparing these means for use should a war break out. Cyber capabilities provide another means of exploiting U.S. and ROK vulnerabilities at relatively low intensity while minimizing risk of retaliation or escalation. In this context, cyber capabilities are logical extensions of both North Korea's peacetime and wartime operations.

1. **North Korea's Strategic Context:** North Korean strategy emphasizes asymmetric and irregular operations in both peacetime and wartime to counter the conventional

military strength of the United States and ROK. North Korea's national strategy has always been defined by the fact that the Korean peninsula is entrenched in a conventional military deadlock. As a result, North Korea's modern peacetime strategy is to launch low-intensity unconventional operations to disrupt the peaceful status quo without escalating the situation to a level the DPRK cannot control or win. However, if a war ever actually breaks out, the Korean People's Army (KPA)'s wartime strategy is to launch extensive irregular operations that exploit U.S. and ROK vulnerabilities and support its regular military operations.

2. **Cyber Capabilities and Asymmetric Strategy:** North Korea sees cyber operations as a relatively low-cost and low-risk means of targeting the vulnerabilities of a state that relies heavily on cyberspace for national and military activity. Disruptive or destructive cyber attacks allow for direct power projection against a distant adversary without physical infiltration or attack. Cyber capabilities are also an effective means to severely disrupt or neutralize the benefits of having a networked military. Issues of attribution and the lack of firmly established norms make it hard for the defender to communicate red lines and threats.

3. **North Korea's Cyber Strategy:** Cyber operations should be thought of as an extension of North Korea's broader national strategy. During peacetime, cyber capabilities allow the DPRK to upset the status quo with little risk of retaliation or immediate operational risk. During wartime, the DPRK would target U.S. and ROK command, control, communications, computers, intelligence, surveillance, and reconnaissance (C4ISR) in support of the DPRK's "quick war, quick end" (속전속결) strategy. North Korean cyber doctrine, if one exists, may be premised on the idea that an extensively networked military is vulnerable to cyber capabilities.

THE ORGANIZATION OF DPRK'S CYBER OPERATIONS

North Korea's cyber operations are not ad hoc, isolated incidents. They are the result of deliberate and organized efforts under the direction of preexisting organizations with established goals and missions that directly support the country's national strategy. Knowing which North Korean organizations plan and execute cyber operations is important because North Korea does not publish its own cyber strategy or doctrine. Examining an organization's historic goals and missions as well as analyzing their known patterns of behavior are the next best option for predicting how North Korea will operationalize cyber capabilities. A top-down perspective on North Korea's cyber operations shows which organizations conduct cyber operations and how strongly they influence operational purposes. The Reconnaissance General Bureau and the General Staff Department of the KPA generally control most of North Korea's known cyber capabilities. These two organizations are responsible for peacetime provocations and wartime disruptive operations, respectively.

1. **The Reconnaissance General Bureau:** The RGB is the primary intelligence and clandestine operations organ known within the North Korean government and is historically associated with peacetime commando raids, infiltrations, disruptions,

and other clandestine operations, including the 2014 Sony Pictures Entertainment attack. The RGB controls the bulk of known DPRK cyber capabilities, mainly under Bureau 121 or its potential successor, the Cyber Warfare Guidance Bureau. There may be a recent or ongoing reorganization within the RGB that promoted Bureau 121 to a higher rank or even established it as the centralized entity for cyber operations. RGB cyber capabilities are likely to be in direct support of the RGB's aforementioned missions. In peacetime, it is also likely to be the more important or active of the two main organizations with cyber capabilities in the DPRK.

2. **The General Staff Department (GSD):** The General Staff Department of the KPA oversees military operations and units, including the DPRK's growing conventional military cyber capabilities. It is tasked with operational planning and ensuring the readiness of the KPA should war break out on the Korean peninsula. It is not currently associated with direct cyber provocations in the same way that the RGB is, but its cyber units may be tasked with preparing disruptive attacks and cyber operations in support of conventional military operations. North Korea's emphasis on combined arms and mixed operations suggests that cyber units will coordinate with or be incorporated as elements within larger conventional military formations.

3. **North Korea's Technology Base:** The DPRK maintains an information technology base that can serve as a general research and development foundation for computer technology and programming. The existence of a software and computer industry means the DPRK's technical industries are not as primitive as many think.

FUTURE THREAT TRENDS FROM DPRK CYBER OPERATIONS

Left unchecked and barring any unpredictable power shift, North Korea is likely to continue to place strategic value in its cyber capabilities. Future North Korean cyber attacks are likely to fall along a spectrum, with one end being continued low-intensity attacks and the other end characterized by high-intensity attacks from an emboldened North Korea. Concurrently, the DPRK will likely deepen the integration of its cyber elements into its conventional military forces. Although North Korea's history of low-intensity provocations makes it more likely that it will continue on the lower end of the spectrum, the United States and ROK should remain wary of the latter possibilities and plan and prepare accordingly.

1. **At one end of the spectrum is a continuation of low-intensity disruptive cyber attacks, possibly with increased frequency.** This may not result in any extensive damage or casualties, but an increase in the frequency of disruptions may result in a general erosion of confidence in key commercial sectors.

2. **At the other end is an emboldened North Korea moving toward higher-intensity attacks, possibly crossing the use of force threshold.** North Korea may be emboldened, either from past success or a miscalculation of its capabilities and adversary resolve, and elevate the intensity of its cyber attacks. This could lead to crossing of the use of force threshold and an escalation of conflict with the United States and ROK.

3. **Cyber capabilities are likely to be increasingly integrated with other operational elements of the DPRK's military.** North Korea has a well-established tradition of irregular operations, provocative behavior, and the integration of these operations with conventional military means. Policymakers should expect a potential combination of cyber operations with diplomatic offensives, psychological operations, military exercises, missile tests, or other provocative behaviors.

4. **Contingency planning for a range of scenarios is necessary.** Although the majority of North Korea's provocations are relatively low intensity, there have also been occasional spikes in intensity, such as the March 2010 sinking of the *Cheonan* and November 2010 shelling of Yeonpyeong Island. These examples mean that contingency plans for high-intensity cyber attacks or a conventional provocation aided by cyber capabilities must also be formulated to mitigate the damage that will likely emerge from an unpredicted escalation.

RECOMMENDATIONS FOR POLICY

There are four main policy objectives for managing the emerging North Korean threat in cyberspace, none of which should be pursued exclusively. Specific policy recommendations for the United States and the U.S.-ROK alliance are made with these four general objectives in mind.

1. Prepare a graduated series of direct responses targeting North Korea's cyber organizations.

2. Curb North Korea's operational freedom in cyberspace.

3. Identify and leverage North Korea's vulnerabilities to maintain strategic balance.

4. Adopt damage mitigation and resiliency measures to ensure that critical systems and networks maintain operational continuity during and after an attack.

Recommendations for the United States

1. **Consider developing a declared policy on the U.S. range of countermeasures for low-intensity cyber attacks qualifying as internationally wrongful acts.** In response to the cyber attack against Sony in November 2014, policymakers did not have an established menu of proportional response options, thus hindering the ability of the United States to respond quickly and send a clear signal. Establishing a declared policy allows for more timely responses and may have deterrent effects. As long as the government is willing and able to execute its own policy, these positives outweigh the negatives of potentially binding one's hands. Sanctioning measures, such as Executive Order 13694 announced on April 1, 2015, have prepared the groundwork for such a policy, but further explicit responses should be set so that U.S. entities are prepared to respond quickly in future crises. Response measures should address low-intensity cyber attacks, so policy should distinguish countermeasures, such as sanctions, from peacetime reprisals, which

would be applicable for attacks that cross use of force or armed-attacked thresholds.

2. **Further implement Executive Orders (EOs) 13687 and 13694 against specific DPRK individuals and/or entities that have engaged in cyber attacks that pose a threat to national security.** The United States now has a basis for sanctioning individuals and entities that engage in or materially support disruptive or destructive cyber operations. The United States should utilize EO 13687 and EO 13694 to further identify and implement sanctions against specific North Korean individuals and entities. This would continue to build a basis for limiting their operational freedom.

3. **Promote strengthening of the international legal and normative base in order to curb North Korea's current operational freedom with a wider range of policy options.** Currently, the international legal and normative basis on state responsibility in cyberspace is weak. Although the United Nations Group of Government Experts (UN GGE) agreed in 2013 and 2015 that states should seek to ensure that their territory is not knowingly being used for international wrongful acts using cyber capabilities, this is far from being practically applied by states. Greater acceptance of this norm, however, could help curb any overseas North Korean activity in support of cyber operations by encouraging states to refrain from knowingly hosting them, and taking appropriate measures when notified of a breach such as through domestic law enforcement or technical cooperation.

4. **Promote policies for international cooperation.** Unilateral action is less effective than deep and broad international cooperation, unless the objective is to purely send a message. The United States will need strong working relationships with other states for both greater enforcement of U.S. sanctions against North Korean individuals and entities and to impose limitations on North Korea's operational freedom. To achieve this, the United States should work with existing allies and partners with an existing common understanding regarding international norms applicable to cyberspace and work jointly to promote their greater adoption at the regional and global level.

Recommendations for the U.S.-ROK Alliance

1. **Develop contingency plans and a menu of corresponding response options for a range of scenarios affected by North Korea's cyber operations.** These scenarios should not be necessarily limited exclusively to cyber operations, as North Korea may launch joint provocations in the future. A range of options from joint U.S.-ROK declaratory statements to operations aimed at degrading North Korean assets should be assessed. War gaming and continued preparation for future crises will continue to be vital. The scope of contingencies considered should go beyond the Korean peninsula and should incorporate the impact on other regional U.S. allies such as Japan, and other important strategic assets in the region such as early warning networks. The U.S.-ROK Cyber Cooperation Working Group, as the current

key bilateral cyber defense dialogue, remains a good mechanism for further concrete discussions.

2. **Consider exploiting North Korea's vulnerability to outside information.** One realistic response option to North Korea's cyber attacks may be to leverage the regime's obsession with tight control on information within the country. This could be considered one of North Korea's largest asymmetric vulnerabilities. Targeting this may be an efficient means of directly influencing North Korean behavior. The continuous introduction of unwanted information into North Korea would create pressure that could be utilized, possibly in conjunction with sanctions or countermeasures, to compel North Korea to end an illicit cyber operation. The recent crisis on the Korean peninsula in August 2015 over South Korean loudspeakers at the demilitarized zone (DMZ) has shown that the North Korean regime may be vulnerable to this measure.

3. **Review the possibility that North Korea's growing cyber power may affect the current strategic balance on the Korean peninsula.** The U.S.-ROK alliance should discuss in subsequent high-level strategic dialogue whether and how North Korea's cyber power may affect the alliance's peacetime and wartime strategic balance. If North Korea's cyber capabilities become increasingly integrated as a supporting element into its conventional military operational planning, the alliance needs to consider how such a situation might augment North Korea's existing military capabilities and how alliance assets might be adversely affected. Examples of possibly affected functions are military command and control, the alliance's air defense networks, and any future missile defense arrangements.

4. **Mitigate vulnerabilities in interoperability arising from the current hub-and-spokes U.S.-ROK alliance structure.** If North Korea's cyber capabilities are increasingly integrated with its conventional military elements, the U.S.-ROK alliance needs to mitigate its inherent vulnerabilities. Alliance networks, military units, and early warning systems must be interoperable and hardened against disruptive cyber operations. South Korea and Japan, even if not directly allied, must cooperate with each other and the United States to track and protect network-dependent assets, such as early warning systems, against cyber attacks. Cyber units in each country must be capable of efficiently communicating and working together to manage threats that stretch beyond just the Korean peninsula.

5. **Encourage greater information-sharing arrangements beyond intelligence and government agencies.** Information sharing is critical in helping each defender gain a more comprehensive picture of the threat and to reduce vulnerabilities accordingly. A more comprehensive knowledge base about North Korea's tactics, techniques, and procedures (TTPs) allows defenders to detect malicious activity at the initial exploitation phase and gives the defender enough time to stop an attack. It also has an added benefit of forcing North Korea to change TTPs more frequently, thus increasing both the expense and risk of each operation. Beyond intelligence

sharing between just intelligence and government agencies, arrangements for sharing more incident response data between computer emergency response teams (CERTs) and computer security incident response teams (CSIRTs) are a valuable option. Additionally, finding mechanisms that incentivize private sector participation is important. Information-sharing mechanisms should also not necessarily be limited to the U.S.-ROK alliance but seek to incorporate a wider cooperative network.

6. **Continue engaging in regional confidence building measures (CBMs) and capacity building efforts to create more common ground on cyber issues in the Asia-Pacific, especially with China.** Both the United States and ROK have been engaged in efforts to implement greater CBMs and capacity building in the Asia-Pacific region. South Korea hosted the Seoul Global Conference on Cyberspace in 2013 and has been active on this issue in regional forums. These include the Association of Southeast Asian Nations (ASEAN) Regional Forum (ARF) and the Asia-Pacific Economic Cooperation (APEC) Telecommunications and Information Working Group (TEL). CBMs provide a basis for increasing transparency and trust, and serve as a starting point for further functional cooperation despite other disagreements. They help buttress the efforts such as the Korea-Japan-China trilateral consultations. Capacity building is closely related to CBMs in that greater domestic technical, legal, and bureaucratic capacity to respond to cyber incidents enables further functional international cooperation. The ROK government's current Northeast Asia Peace and Cooperation Initiative (NAPCI), which seeks to increase cooperation in the region by focusing on issue-specific dialogues, could further focus on cyber issues by identifying and implementing CBMs and capacity building efforts.

7. **Leverage existing bilateral coordination on international norms and standards as a platform for further adoption regionally and globally.** Over the past few years, the United States and ROK have been involved in multiagency bilateral cyber policy consultations that resulted in a common understanding regarding international norms about cyberspace. North Korea's cyber threat has provided a concrete situation around which norms could be further refined, and these efforts should not be thought of as just limited to the Korean peninsula. The United States and ROK should further coordinate on international cyber policy in regional and global forums in order to place further weight on such norms.

1 | Strategic Context

DPRK Military and Political Strategy

This section provides a brief introduction to how the DPRK's military and political strategies have evolved since the end of the 1950–1953 Korean War. In order to examine the strategic motivations behind the DPRK's current military and political use of cyber capabilities and to think about how the DPRK's cyber capabilities will affect the overall strategic balance in the Korean peninsula and beyond, it is important to first understand how the DPRK's strategic goals have changed over time and how it has employed the means at its disposal to meet this end. Two distinct aspects of the DPRK's strategy are discussed: the development of its peacetime asymmetric strategy, characterized by investing in unconventional military capabilities and engaging in frequent low-intensity provocations short of war, and its older conventional war strategy aimed at fighting a blitzkrieg-style of quick, decisive war in the Korean peninsula.

DPRK ASYMMETRIC STRATEGY[1]

One of the defining characteristics of the DPRK's modern military strategy is its focus on developing an asymmetric advantage over the ROK and the United States, which is its principal ally. An asymmetric strategy is when an actor develops means specifically to target vulnerabilities of the adversary rather than to confront the adversary head on.[2] The objective of an asymmetric strategy is usually not the total defeat of the adversary, but to undermine the adversary's will by disruption, destruction, exhaustion, or coercion. An asymmetric strategy is not necessarily only tied to the choice of the means employed (i.e., nuclear weapons), but also encompasses conventional weapons (i.e., artillery) used in unconventional ways.

The DPRK has increasingly relied on an asymmetric military strategy over the past few decades, largely stemming from the increasingly difficult military and economic position the DPRK has found itself. Since the end of the Korean War, the Korean People's Army (KPA)'s main stated objective has been to reunify the peninsula under the DPRK's rule.

---

1. In this discussion of strategy and doctrine, asymmetric refers to a capability that does not necessarily have an immediate identical response, specifically offensive cyber operations conducted against an opponent that does not or cannot respond with cyber operations. In contrast, symmetric would be something such as ground forces responding to ground forces. When offensive cyber capabilities are demonstrated by both sides with some degree of normalcy, they would cease being asymmetric.

2. Bruce W. Bennett, Christopher P. Twomey, and Gregory F. Treverton, *What Are Asymmetric Strategies?* (Santa Monica, CA: RAND Publishing, 1999).

While the military balance on the Korean peninsula favored the DPRK for the first few decades after the Korean War, by the late 1980s the balance had reversed. The KPA's objective became increasingly unattainable as the ROK's economy grew rapidly and the DPRK's economy stagnated, resulting in a wide discrepancy in military budgets. Even though the DPRK invests a large proportion of its gross national income (GNI) in the military, fighting and winning a conventional war on the Korean peninsula soon became unrealistic, if not impossible, for the DPRK.[3] The disparity grew even more with the end of the Cold War, which resulted in decreased Russian and Chinese patronage of the DPRK. Meanwhile, the United States maintained its presence in the ROK.

Under these circumstances, it became apparent that a more realistic way of attaining an advantage on the Korean peninsula was through means other than conventional military action. Acquiring irregular and asymmetric warfare capabilities became the logical path for the DPRK. Thus the DPRK invested in relatively low-cost (compared to full modernization of its vast conventional military) but highly effective systems such as nuclear weapons, ballistic missiles, and a robust special forces command capable of acting outside of the conventional military deadlock. The DPRK maintains one of the largest special forces in the world. These investments allowed it to continue to pose an asymmetric, coercive threat against the United States and ROK despite having a conventionally inferior military force.

The pursuit of irregular and asymmetric military capabilities ties in deeply to the DPRK's development of cyber capabilities. What started as commando raids, assassination attempts, bombings, and sabotage gradually gave way to new forms of provocations as these methods came to be widely criticized by the international community and specific rules of engagement were developed to counter these actions. Cyber attacks in this context effectively replace or, at a minimum, augment existing provocative capabilities because retaliation is difficult and similar damaging effects can be achieved at relatively low cost and operational risk. Crime, espionage, sabotage, and coercion can all be perpetrated via cyberspace, with the right training and infrastructure.

A HISTORY OF PROVOCATIONS SHORT OF WAR

One manifestation of the DPRK's asymmetric strategy has been its frequent provocations against the ROK and United States. Historically, the DPRK has pursued various means to exert its influence and will upon the ROK without necessarily engaging in conventional military confrontations. Most of these provocations relied on irregular and asymmetric means and fell outside of the framework of traditional military activity.[4] By using limited force that falls below the threshold of triggering armed conflict yet still effective enough to

---

3. Yang-ju Kwon, *The Comprehension of North Korean Military* (Seoul: Korea Institute of Defense Analyses, 2010), 163.
4. CSIS Korea Chair, *Record of North Korea's Major Conventional Provocations since 1960s* (Washington, DC: Center for Strategic and International Studies, 2010), http://csis.org/publication/record-north-koreas-major -conventional-provocations-1960s.

disrupt the status quo and bring about general unrest, the DPRK has been able to coerce the ROK despite having weaker conventional forces.[5]

One of the first major provocations was the 1968 Blue House Raid, during which a team of commandos infiltrated across the DMZ with the goal of assassinating Park Chung-hee, South Korea's president. The assassination attempt culminated in a firefight a few hundred meters from President Park's residence. This provocation is typically associated with the Ministry of People's Armed Forces Reconnaissance Bureau, a predecessor to the modern Reconnaissance General Bureau (RGB), an organization that will be discussed later.

In 1983, the Reconnaissance Bureau attempted to assassinate President Chun Doo-hwan during an official visit to the Martyr's Mausoleum in Rangoon, Burma. The Reconnaissance Bureau planted and detonated a bomb at the site, killing several South Korean cabinet officials and Burmese government officials, though Chun himself escaped.[6]

In 1987, possibly in retaliation for bitter and embarrassing negotiations regarding the upcoming 1988 Seoul Olympics, two North Korean agents planted and detonated a bomb on a Korean airliner, killing all 115 passengers aboard. This event is associated with the Korean Worker's Party Office 35, specifically its leadership.[7] This is another organization that was incorporated into the current RGB.

More recently, a DPRK semi-submersible torpedoed the ROK Navy Pohang-class corvette *Cheonan* in March 2010 and fired artillery pieces in November 2010 against Yeonpyeong Island, resulting in several civilian and military casualties and the deaths of 46 ROK sailors. While Yeonpyeong Island represented a very serious and arguably conventional military provocation, many argue that the *Cheonan* was a more asymmetric provocation and was most likely sunk by the RGB, which is currently the primary clandestine operations organization within the North Korean government.[8]

Since the end of the Korean War there have also been smaller asymmetric provocations, including less violent commando raids and submarine infiltrations, infrastructure sabotage and bombings, and the digging of infiltration tunnels beneath the DMZ. A more detailed timeline and list of these provocations appears in *Record of North Korea's Major Conventional Provocations since 1960s*, published in 2010.[9]

This brief history of some of the DPRK's belligerent behavior shows some of its use of asymmetric operations. As long as the Korean peninsula remains a zero-sum game for

5. Victor D. Cha, "Hawk Engagement and Preventive Defense on the Korean Peninsula," *International Security* 27, no. 1 (Summer 2002): 40–78.

6. Sang-sook Chun, "Rangoon Bombing Incident," National Archives of Korea, December 1, 2006, http://www.archives.go.kr/next/search/listSubjectDescription.do?id=002844&pageFlag=.

7. Joseph S. Bermudez, "A New Emphasis on Operations Against South Korea?," 38 North Special Report, U.S. Korea Institute at School of Advanced International Studies (SAIS), 2010, http://38north.org/wp-content/uploads/2010/06/38north_SR_Bermudez2.pdf.

8. So-hyun Kim, "'Reconnaissance General Bureau Is Heart of N.K. Terrorism,'" *Korea Herald*, May 26, 2010, http://www.koreaherald.com/view.php?ud=20100526000675.

9. CSIS Korea Chair, *Record of North Korea's Provocations*.

legitimacy and control, the buildup around the DMZ prevents conventional action from solving the problem of control on the Korean peninsula and other means must be used to attack the opponent. The DPRK has invested in midget submarines, converted civilian boats to disguise naval operations, and, most noticeably and publicly, nuclear weapons and ballistic missiles.

The DPRK has pursued nuclear weapons as the classic asymmetric weapon. It provides for deterrence against the United States and ROK. It also means the DPRK can devote less attention and resources to its conventional military strength. Ballistic missiles, as well, allow for delivery of conventional or weapons of mass destruction (WMD) warheads to anywhere in the ROK in half an hour or less. These looming and threatening DPRK capabilities require incredibly large financial investments to symmetrically counter.

The DPRK looks for advantages that it can capitalize to both undermine the ROK/U.S. position and defend itself from the ROK and United States. Over the years it has pursued capabilities and performed operations that show an interest in continuing to attack the ROK and United States in ways that neither country may expect or have a reliable defense for or counter against.

Cyber capabilities offer one of the best investments for an isolated state that is looking for the capability to coerce, compel, harass, spy, and raise capital through legal and illicit means. All of the main asymmetric capabilities that the DPRK has pursued can be greatly augmented and aided by the military use of cyberspace.

DPRK'S CONVENTIONAL WARFARE STRATEGY

Another important concept in the DPRK's military strategy is the concept of blitzkrieg[10] warfare on the Korean peninsula. The DPRK's reliance on provocations as a tool for coercion during peacetime does not mean that it has abandoned preparation for the possibility of conducting a conventional war on the Korean peninsula. Contrary to conventional wisdom, the DPRK is tenaciously modernizing its military and maintaining readiness to the best extent possible.

Though this is now a less realistic strategy than it has been in 1960s or 1970s, North Korea's war scenario involves fighting a quick war supported by irregular and special forces from both front and rear, in which the DPRK aggressively tries to eject U.S. forces from the peninsula before reinforcements arrive and seize key strategic locations in South Korea. The DPRK can then present a fait accompli at the negotiating table without necessarily achieving total victory. In this context, the DPRK's growing cyber capabilities, if successfully integrated with its blitzkrieg-style strategy, can enhance DPRK's maneuver operations by disrupting the ROK's command and control, allowing quick penetration by the DPRK's mechanized forces.

---

10. The Korean term 속전속결 literally translates as "quick war, quick end." Very similar in concept to blitzkrieg, a series of swift tactical engagements support a greater operation that induces systemic collapse of opposing forces and a relatively swift strategic victory before the tempo of warfare slows to a grinding attritive pace.

Offensively, the DPRK maintains a strategy aimed at fighting a high-intensity, short-duration war in which the southern half of the peninsula is quickly isolated and overwhelmed before the United States has a chance to send in substantial reinforcements.[11] Such a strategy relies heavily on maneuver warfare, where mechanized forces quickly penetrate enemy defenses, race to the rear, and isolate and destroy defending forces while irregular and light infantry infiltrate and disrupt enemy rear areas. Among many of the components required for successful maneuver operations, tempo is an important element.

In the DPRK's ideal warfighting scenario, it would fight a quick and overwhelming war in which both the conventional and irregular forces would be employed against both front and rear areas.[12] A swift and aggressive push southward with a simultaneous rear-area invasion by irregular light infantry forces would be aimed at disrupting and distracting the ROK and U.S. military. This peninsular blitzkrieg would eliminate the U.S. foothold on the peninsula, subsequently increasing the costs and difficulty of retaking the peninsula.

In theory, by having a faster decision cycle than the adversary, fast-moving mechanized forces can maneuver quicker than the defense is able to confront and destroy the threat. In a conventional war, the role of the KPA's large special forces and light infantry would be to preoccupy and disrupt South Korean forces while its KPA main forces move southward. In this context, the DPRK has the potential to integrate its electronic and cyber warfare capabilities into its broader conventional warfare strategy to disrupt the ROK and U.S. command and control during an attack.

A 2014 report from the ROK Ministry of Unification states:

> North Korea's military strategy is based on fighting a short war based on blitz strategy (속전속결). Taking into account the geography of the Korean peninsula and North Korea's capacity to wage war, the strategy focuses on surprise attack from both front and rear in order to create chaos in the initial stages of war, allowing deep infiltration by fast-moving armored units, occupying South Korea before U.S. reinforcements could arrive.
>
> Until the mid-70s, North Korea focused on enhancing capabilities in terms of number of forces rather than the quality of weaponry. North Korea especially focused on enhancing capabilities to conduct simultaneous frontal and rear operations, achieving operational depth fast, and surprise first attack. By the end of 1980s, North Korea acquired the ability to independently conduct 2–3 months of battle by forward-deploying forces and artillery and forming mechanized units and special forces.[13]

---

11. Sanghee Lee, "Thoughts on an 'Initiative Strategy' for the Comprehensive Management of North Korea" (Washington, DC: Brookings Institution, 2010), http://www.brookings.edu/research/papers/2010/04/north-korea-lee.

12. James M. Minnich, *The North Korean People's Army: Origins and Current Tactics* (Annapolis, MD: Naval Institute Press, 2005), 73–74.

13. "Understanding North Korea" (Seoul: Education Center for Unification, 2014), http://www.unikorea.go.kr/content.do?cmsid=1762&mode=view&page=&cid=41603.

The DPRK's strategy incorporates the integration of asymmetric elements of warfare into its otherwise conventional operations. This is sometimes referred to as a mixed or combined tactics[14] or joint operations.[15] This concept is somewhat related to the U.S. concept of hybrid warfare.[16] While respective utilities of the Korean People's Navy and Air Force in a real war are questionable, the combination or mixing of standard ground force units with asymmetric capabilities such as ballistic missiles, special forces, and cyber operations could be fairly potent. The DPRK leadership has notably emphasized the importance of high-tech capabilities in modern warfare and the importance of integrating these capabilities into a modern fighting force, which will be addressed later in this chapter.

One of the most important elements of this type of maneuver warfare is the advantage provided by a strong surprise attack,[17] similar to what started the Korean War. A surprise attack maximizes the chance that the attacking forces would penetrate enemy defenses before the adversary has time to react effectively. A surprise attack would employ the DPRK's large, yet aging, conventional and regular forces, as well as its very large irregular and asymmetric forces. Whereas the Korean War started with conventional formations pushing southward, any new invasion would involve new technologies that enable DPRK deep strikes against ROK operational areas and the disruption of ROK and U.S. logistical and information networks. The DPRK has particularly focused on investing new technologies that would support fast wars.[18] Although a conventional warfare strategy seems unrealistic today, the ROK Ministry of National Defense, along with numerous Korean and American scholars and officials, maintain that the DPRK continues to espouse this concept as its strategy and has made military acquisitions to this end.

Understanding this background in DPRK military strategy is crucial for understanding how North Korea might incorporate its growing cyber capabilities into its broader military strategy. Recent literature, drawing lessons from the 2013 DarkSeoul (3.20 attack in South Korea) attack or the 2014 Sony Pictures Entertainment incident, points out the possibility of the DPRK using cyber capabilities as strategic attacks, but this literature does not adequately entertain the possibility of cyber capabilities potentially changing the military balance during a conventional war.

Lessons of recent wars such as Operation Desert Storm indicate that timely and accurate battlefield information has become crucial at the tactical and operational level. Militaries are increasingly relying on digital means to create, transmit, store, and modify such information. For example, militaries with advanced air, missile, and general long-range strike capabilities require timely and accurate data regarding targets. One of the cheaper

---

14. Minnich, *North Korean People's Army*, 73.
15. Heung-kwang Kim, "Responses and Strategies against North Korea's Cyber Information Warfare" (Seoul: North Korea Intellectuals Solidarity, 2010), http://www.nkis.kr/board.php?board=nkisb501&page=1&sort=hit&command=body&no=3.
16. A hybrid war is a conflict that combines conventional forces, irregular forces, and asymmetric capabilities, including cyber operations.
17. Kim, "Responses and Strategies."
18. "Understanding North Korea," 135.

and more effective ways to neutralize such capabilities would be to disrupt or destroy data or the network transmitting this data, rather than to develop expensive weapons systems to counter them. Another example is the centrality of command and control as combined arms warfare has become the norm. Modern operations almost always require timely and accurate coordination between different arms components, and sometimes require extensive data processing at headquarters. The disruption or destruction of such command and control capabilities would in some instances buy enough time for the offense.

FINAL NOTES

The array of forces on the Korean peninsula since 1950 has made unrealistic the notion of fighting another all-out war, though conventional defense planning still continues. DPRK strategists have tried to gain an advantage despite this stalemate and the U.S.-ROK alliance's superior capabilities by adopting an asymmetric strategy that uses coercive actions short of full-scale war. Their means of coercion have diversified over time, from commando raids and bombings to special forces and nuclear weapons. By exploiting the fact that the DPRK and ROK place different values in maintaining a peaceful status quo, the DPRK has been able to threaten its stronger counterpart though cycles of provocations.

There is reason to believe that DPRK's growing cyber capabilities would serve as another instrument in its toolbox of provocations. The emphasis its conventional war strategy places on fighting a blitzkrieg-style war on the peninsula raises the question of whether the DPRK will, or already has, incorporated cyber capabilities to this end. Considering the evolution of the DPRK's military and political strategy, the state's investment in cyber capabilities not only makes logical and strategic sense, but also indicates that there is a strong motivation by the central leadership to continue to invest in and nurture this capability over time.

In short, in peacetime, the DPRK has both a history of and incentive toward asymmetric provocations. The status quo cannot be revised via direct, conventional military confrontation, but it can be slightly upset with asymmetric provocations that fall short of war as these can be difficult to respond to and prevent. In planning for war, it has an incentive toward asymmetric disruptive operations, especially aimed at disrupting its opponents' superior technological advantage. Overall, the DPRK pursues capabilities that allow it to act unexpectedly or in a way that is difficult to contain and respond to.

Strategic Use of Cyberspace

This section provides a brief introduction to how cyberspace and cyber capabilities have been used for strategic ends. It focuses on key characteristics of cyberspace, selected past cases of cyberspace used in a strategic context, and the potential strategic advantages of leveraging cyberspace in conflict. This section aims to establish an introductory context for those less familiar with cyberspace and cyber capabilities, to create a common understanding for subsequent discussion on North Korea's cyber strategy.

CHARACTERISTICS OF CYBERSPACE

The term *cyberspace* is often defined and used in various different ways. For purposes of this report, cyberspace is defined as part of an information environment used to create, store, modify, transfer, delete, and exploit information by the transmission of signals through the electromagnetic spectrum via a collection of interconnected systems comprising electronic hardware, software, and its supporting physical infrastructure.

Physically, cyberspace consists of hardware components used in building a network, such as routers, servers, and computers, and the infrastructure that allows these components to be connected, such as fiber-optic cables, local area network (LAN) cables, or wireless technology. These hardware components are geopolitically defined and usually subject to national jurisdiction. Although often not included in a definition of cyberspace, in the context of national security some states will also put into consideration enabling infrastructure such as telecommunication systems and electrical grids. These hardware components are connected in a network by software components allowing information to be sent and received in packets according to network protocols, such as the ISO/OSI Reference Model or the TCP/IP model.[19]

A functional description of cyberspace is contested across different states and organizations. In the most basic sense, cyberspace concerns the information within or transferred through networked computer systems and the human interaction with other humans or information via these networks. From this point, organizations have different notions about the activities in and through cyberspace that ought to be regulated and/or controlled, and such notions are reflected in their respective definitions. Most importantly, some will describe cyberspace as simply a networked environment, placing emphasis on the infrastructure and connectivity, while others will explicitly include the information content portion in their definitions, which helps the organization to regulate or influence related concepts such as intellectual property, freedom of speech, and privacy.[20] Regardless of such differences, for purposes of this report both the content and the environment are considered to be essential functional features of cyberspace.

Several major characteristics of cyberspace are relevant. First, cyberspace allows users to transmit vast quantities of information efficiently and quickly. Communications are not merely point-to-point or broadcast but utilize packet switching, whereby information is broken down into small blocks based on a destination address and then sent through multiple paths. The communication path is not dedicated, but variable and distributed. This feature has allowed for a new paradigm of information exchange.

---

19. For a deeper discussion on a definition of cyberspace, refer to Daniel T. Kuehl, "Chapter 2: From Cyberspace to Cyberpower: Defining the Problem," in *Cyberpower and National Security*, ed. Franklin D. Kramer et. al. (Washington, DC: National Defense University, 2009).

20. Melissa E. Hathaway and Alexander Klimburg, "1.2 Cyber Terms and Definitions," in *National Cybersecurity Framework Manual*, ed. Alexander Klimburg (Tallinn, Estonia: NATO CCD COE Publications, 2012).

Second, users have so far enjoyed a large degree of anonymity. Many networked systems, including the Internet, have not been designed with security or identity in mind. Despite the existence of some identification features such as IP addresses and media access control (MAC) addresses, it is often difficult to track the source of an activity in cyberspace back to its origin. It is also difficult to establish a connection between the actual physical/legal identity of the person and his/her persona in cyberspace. Recently, however, various tools and techniques have emerged to manage the attribution problem better. The severity of the attribution problem varies depending on the malicious actor and the type of cyber activity.[21] Still, as a general trend attribution still remains time consuming, costly, and often requires cooperation between authorities in different countries.

Third, unlike other operational domains, cyberspace is a man-made domain where much of the hardware and software building blocks can be modified and reconfigured. This means that networks and systems can be rebuilt and redesigned in more than one way depending on an organization's priorities and needs, though cost and path dependency remain as obstacles.

OPERATIONS IN AND THROUGH CYBERSPACE

The history of cyber operations is still elusive and ill-defined, as cyber operations themselves are still largely clandestine in nature. Not only are the details of cyber means being utilized as part of a military operation not readily available to the public, even the most well-known cases have yet to be weaved into a coherent, thematic history of cyber warfare. Categorizing cyber warfare into existing frameworks have also been difficult. While cyber warfare shares some lineage with information warfare (IW) and electronic warfare (EW), cyber capabilities have also been used in entirely different strategic contexts, including sabotage and limited strategic attacks. Nonetheless, particular cyber incidents in the past two decades have been consistently referred to as being significant to an understanding of cyber warfare. The incidents discussed below are generally regarded as salient cases contributing to an evolving concept of cyber warfare.

One useful framework for thinking about how operations in and through cyberspace have been conducted is to determine what features of cyberspace have been targeted and for what military or political objective they have been targeted. Generally, cyber operations have targeted the computer system itself, the information resident in it, or both. The disruption or destruction of these targets have either been the final military objective or were targeted in support of other conventional military means to achieve another objective.

Cyber warfare, which was commonly referred to as information war or net-centric war in the 1990s, has strategic roots in information warfare. Operation Desert Storm demonstrated the immense advantages of having a networked military that had near real-time

---

21. U.S. House Science and Technology Committee, *Untangling Attribution: Moving to Accountability in Cyberspace*, 111th Cong., 2nd sess., July 15, 2010, 4.

situational awareness that boosted the effects of combined arms and maneuver warfare.[22] Digital communications provided superior C4ISR, and combined with extensive EW operations and early air superiority, coalition forces easily destroyed Iraqi forces. Colonel John Warden, architect of the strategic air campaign during Operation Desert Storm, claimed that "with fewer than 1 percent of the bombs dropped on Vietnam, the coalition imposed strategic and operational paralysis on Iraq."[23] Coalition success was so great that net-centric warfare was soon dubbed as a revolution in military affairs (RMA).[24] Much of this success was due to the dual role of advanced precision-guided munitions (PGMs) coupled with access to timely and accurate targeting information. Information in war has always been important, but after Operation Desert Storm it became an even more integral part of modern warfare.

Among other states that began a deeper study of the role of cyber capabilities in warfare, the People's Liberation Army (PLA) of China in particular sought an informatization or informationalization of its military, under a broader objective of achieving information dominance.[25] Complementing this effort were strategies to undermine any adversary's utilization of cyberspace in conflict. *Unrestricted Warfare*,[26] written in 1999 by two PLA officers, explained how states can overcome a high-tech, conventionally superior military by resorting to weapons and tactics outside of the traditional rules of conflict, including cyber warfare. These types of works demonstrated the importance of the strategic use of cyberspace in modern warfare, and in turn a need to secure command of this domain as a military objective. Chinese conceptualization of the cyber domain, however, slightly differs from the U.S. conceptualization because its cyber capabilities fall under a larger concept of "information operations" that encompasses electronic warfare and psychological operations.[27] Network defense and attack is certainly a portion of China's cyber strategy, but information resident in the networks and systems is also regarded as a crucial element of warfare.

There have been several past cases where cyber warfare has been combined with conventional means in a military operation. The most prominent of this case is Russia's use of cyber capabilities during the 2008 Russo-Georgian War, in integration with the efforts of conventional combat forces.[28] Attacks initially involved DDoS attacks and website deface-

---

22. Lawrence Freedman, "The Revolution in Military Affairs," in *Strategy: A History* (New York: Oxford University Press, 2013), 215–236.

23. Gregory J. Rattray, *Strategic Warfare in Cyberspace* (Cambridge, MA: MIT Press, 2001), 91.

24. Freedman, "Revolution."

25. Bryan Krekel, Patton Adams, and George Bakos, *Occupying the Information High Ground: Chinese Capabilities for Computer Network Operations and Cyber Espionage* (Washington, DC: Northrop Grumman Corp, 2012), http://nsarchive.gwu.edu/NSAEBB/NSAEBB424/docs/Cyber-066.pdf.

26. Liang Qiao and Xiangsui Wang, *Unrestricted Warfare* (Beijing: PLA Literature and Arts Publishing House, 1999).

27. Amy Chang, *Warring State: China's Cybersecurity Strategy* (Washington, DC: Center for New American Security, 2014).

28. For an in-depth treatment of Russia's utilization of cyber capabilities during the 2008 Russo-Georgian War, please refer to David Hollis, "Cyberwar Case Study: Georgia 2008," *SWJ Blog, Small Wars Journal*, January 6, 2011, http://smallwarsjournal.com/blog/journal/docs-temp/639-hollis.pdf; Andreas Hagen, *The Russo-Georgian War of 2008: The Role of the Cyber Attacks in the Conflict* (Fairfax, VA: AFCEA International, 2012), http://www.afcea.org/committees/cyber/documents/TheRusso-GeorgianWar2008.pdf; John Bumgarner and

ments against government and media websites, which subsequently expanded to a wider target list including the websites of more government agencies, financial institutions, educational institutions, and a Georgian hacking forum.[29] The objective of such attacks, especially during the initial phases of conflict, seems to have been to disrupt national decisionmaking and effective communication between the government and the public. These disruptions caused by cyber capabilities, while limited in damage and relatively unsophisticated in methods, may support the main warfighting forces to have greater operational freedom by disrupting the opponent's decision cycle.[30] It is uncertain, however, whether Russia's cyber operations were actually integral to the success of the overall military mission.

Operation Orchard is a more specific case where the military use of cyber capabilities was integral to the success of a military operation. In September 2007, the Israeli Air Force conducted an airstrike against Syria's al-Kibar nuclear reactor site.[31] In this operation, several Israeli non-stealth aircraft were able to fly into Syrian airspace absolutely unimpeded in coordination with on-the-ground special forces units.[32] It was later discovered that the Israelis may have penetrated the Syrian air defense network beforehand and compromised its radar systems.[33] Though the exact method of the cyber attack is unknown, it is possible that a combination of electronic and cyber warfare means were used to render Syria's radar useless. The most important lesson from this operation was that the Syrians were not aware that their radar had been compromised, which allowed Israeli aircraft to operate within Syrian airspace unimpeded. Had the Israelis used other means to disable the radar, for example, by firing missiles or sending jamming signals, this would have alerted the Syrians and exposed the operation. Operation Orchard demonstrated that disrupting enemy C4ISR, especially in a surreptitious manner through cyber means, can be an integral part of a military mission.

During the War in Afghanistan, the United States utilized unspecified types of cyber attacks to gain an advantage over its adversaries, though there are minimal details available publicly. A short statement from Lieutenant General Richard Mills gives some insight into cyber operations in Afghanistan. At a 2012 conference, he stated that his team "was able to get inside [the enemy's] nets, infect [the enemy's] command-and-control, and in fact defend myself against [the enemy's] almost constant incursions to get inside my wire, to affect my operations."[34] This statement indicates that the U.S. military is actively supporting

---

Scott Borg, *Overview by the US-CCU of the Cyber Campaign against Georgia in August of 2008* (Washington, DC: U.S. Cyber Consequences Unit, 2009), http://www.registan.net/wp-content/uploads/2009/08/US-CCU-Georgia -Cyber-Campaign-Overview.pdf; and E. Lincoln Bonner III, "Cyber Power in 21st-Century Joint Warfare," *Joint Force Quarterly* 74 (2014): 102–109.

29. Bumgarner and Borg, *Overview by the US-CCU.*

30. Bonner, "Cyber Power."

31. Erich Follath and Holger Stark, "The Story of 'Operation Orchard': How Israel Destroyed Syria's Al Kibar Nuclear Reactor," Spiegel Online, November 2, 2009, http://www.spiegel.de/international/world/the-story -of-operation-orchard-how-israel-destroyed-syria-s-al-kibar-nuclear-reactor-a-658663.html.

32. Thomas Rid, *Cyber War Will Not Take Place* (London: Oxford University Press, 2013), 42.

33. Ibid.

34. Tom Gjelten, "Pentagon Goes on the Offensive against Cyberattacks," NPR, February 11, 2013, http:// www.npr.org/2013/02/11/171677247/pentagon-goes-on-the-offensive-against-cyber-attacks.

and integrating its direct combat activities with support in the form of network penetration and exploitation, showing that cyber warfare capabilities can serve to be crucial in the battlefield where situational awareness is key.

On the other hand, cyber capabilities also have been used to conduct strategic attacks or sabotage, albeit relatively limited in impact so far, because the disruption or destruction of the target was not to aid another conventional operation but to achieve a specific strategic objective. For the cases discussed above, the objective has been to use cyber means to deny or disrupt an adversary's access or use of cyberspace. The following cases, however, use cyber means to conduct attacks through cyberspace to disrupt or destroy a physical target.

In terms of impact, the most destructive cyber attacks have been those that target industrial control systems (ICS) and its supervisory control and data acquisition (SCADA) software. The earliest known incident is the alleged 1982 U.S. Central Intelligence Agency (CIA) sabotage of the Soviet Trans-Siberian pipeline infrastructure's SCADA system. The United States, working clandestinely with a Canadian supplier, allegedly compromised the pipeline system's SCADA software by inserting a logic bomb. The software was then installed on the Soviet pipeline. When the logic bomb caused the programmable logic controllers (PLCs) to fail, the pipeline exploded, an event allegedly visible from space.[35] This is the first known case of a supply chain attack. It demonstrated that a strategically valuable infrastructure could be targeted and destroyed without the physical movement of armed forces and without serious apparent repercussions due to the difficulties in ascertaining attribution.

Another incident demonstrated that SCADA systems can be compromised without physical compromise of the supply chain. In 2000, a disgruntled former contractor caused around 800,000 liters of sewage to overflow at the Maroochy Water Services in Australia.[36] The attacker, having worked for a contractor company that supplied SCADA equipment for the plant, had insider knowledge about the systems. With a radio transmitter and a laptop, he successfully issued false radio commands from outside, which caused pumps to stop running, disabled alarms, and prevented communication between the central computer to the stations. As SCADA systems began to be connected to the Internet for ease of use, the vulnerability of these systems increased.

Others soon developed more sophisticated ways to exploit this vulnerability. In 2007, the U.S. Department of Homeland Security and the Idaho National Laboratory successfully conducted Project Aurora, a test in which a hacking team compromised an isolated electrical generator in California after successfully hacking into its SCADA network and controlling its PLCs remotely, causing turbines to spin faster than normal. The relative ease with

---

35. Thomas C. Reed, *At the Abyss: An Insider's History of the Cold War* (New York, NY: Presidio Press, 2005).

36. For an in-depth case study, please refer to Marshall Abrams and Joe Weiss, "Malicious Control System Cyber Security Attack Case Study—Maroochy Water Services, Australia" (Gaithersburg, MD: National Institute of Standards and Technology, 2008), http://csrc.nist.gov/groups/SMA/fisma/ics/documents/Maroochy-Water -Services-Case-Study_report.pdf.

which the attack was executed, the remote and discreet nature of the attack, and the high strategic value of the targets led to the conclusion that the protection of critical infrastructure was vital to national security. However, the test also demonstrated that the same method could also be used to target enemy infrastructures, possibly with significantly lower operational risk than physical infiltration.

The discovery of an operation dubbed Olympic Games became the first publicly known case of using such capabilities for strategic ends. The accidental discovery of the Stuxnet worm in summer 2010 revealed an extensive operation targeting Iran's Natanz nuclear enrichment facility.[37] Among its many functions, Stuxnet exploited four zero-day vulnerabilities and specifically targeted a Siemens SCADA system used in Natanz, indicating significant planning and organization behind the operation. For years the worm issued false commands to the PLCs controlling the centrifuges, causing them to spin out of control. The goal was not to destroy all of the centrifuges but to discreetly cause a portion of them to fail in succession, causing Iranian engineers to believe it was a system failure. The utility of this operation is debated; some claim that it has set back Iran's nuclear program several years, while others claim that its strategic impact was minimal. Contrary to conventional wisdom, the operation was neither cheap nor easy. It demonstrated that the most sophisticated cyber operations require significant technical organization and intelligence capabilities. Nonetheless, the incident was the first case in which a cyber weapon caused notable physical destruction in a strategic context.

Another class of destructive malware that emerged in recent years is the Wiper malware, in which computers of a target network are rendered useless. Several attacks shared similar methods in that they specifically overwrote the master boot record (MBR) of computers hard drives, which then needed to be physically replaced in many cases. The first known case of such an attack was Shamoon in 2012, where about three-quarters of Saudi Aramco's 30,000 computers were shut down with a malware that had a hard drive wiping function similar to that seen in one of Flame's modules. Although there was no physical destruction and business halted for slightly over two weeks, the incident was significant because the effect was semi-permanent, which could be critical if operations need to be continuous. Similar methods were used in March 2013 to wipe the hard drives of major South Korean banks and media outlets, as well as in the cyber attack against Sony in November 2014.

The incidents discussed above illustrate that despite a relatively short history, actors around the world have made deliberate attempts to use cyber capabilities for political and/or military ends. However, the majority of the discussion has focused on the means—malware analysis, attack vectors, impact of the attack, technical attribution. There have been limited efforts to discuss an actor's cyber strategy—*how* the perpetrator is using the

---

37. For more detailed accounts of Olympic Games, refer to Kim Zetter, *Countdown to Zero Day: Stuxnet and the Launch of the World's First Digital Weapon* (New York: Crown, 2014); and David E. Sanger, "Obama Order Sped Up Wave of Cyberattacks against Iran," *New York Times*, June 1, 2012, http://www.nytimes.com/2012/06/01/world/middleeast/obama-ordered-wave-of-cyberattacks-against-iran.html?_r=0.

cyber means at its disposal to achieve what it wants, and *how* this fits into the perpetrator's larger strategic objectives. Like traditional conflict, the deliberate development and use of cyber capabilities are seldom acts of random violence. An understanding of the motivations behind these incidents is imperative to delineate patterns, analyze how capabilities might evolve, and figure out how to counter attacks.

CYBER CAPABILITIES AND ASYMMETRIC ADVANTAGES

As past cases have shown, the ability to disrupt or destroy one or more of the elements comprising cyberspace, including the information, software, and the physical infrastructure, has been put to strategic use by both state and non-state actors. Although both the strong and weak have utilized and incorporated cyber capabilities in conflict, for the purposes of this report it is worth exploring how cyber capabilities can pose an asymmetric threat, especially by an actor with inferior conventional military strength.

Generally, the offense has an advantage over defense in cyberspace, though this is not necessarily true in all cases. The key disadvantage for the defense is that the information asymmetry is severe. The attacker has great freedom choosing when and how to compromise a system while the defender is forced to continuously defend all possible vectors and assets. This makes the defense costly and cumbersome, usually to the point that not everyone can afford it. Furthermore, cyber defense is still often static, relying on firewalls and intrusion detection systems that fail to filter out attacks using unknown malware or stolen legitimate credentials. The lack of information sharing among defenders, though it has gotten better recently, allows the attacker to reuse similar tools and tactics on other targets. Although the most sophisticated attacks such as Stuxnet take considerable time, cost, and organization, many attacks that do not reach this threshold are relatively cheap, easy, and repeatable.

Cyber capabilities can be an effective means to neutralize or suppress the benefits of advanced weaponry and combined arms. Because modern military systems rely extensively on digital communications and data storage, the disruption or destruction of these functions can be crucial in an operation. For example, modern air operations often rely on beyond visual range (BVR) systems and sensors, and early warning radars are crucial for missile defense. Much like jamming in EW, for a weak military power it is much more cost-effective to try to neutralize these functions than to invest in modern weapons systems. For example, lessons from Operation Orchard tell us that effective suppression of enemy air defenses by cyber means allows even a nonstealth aircraft to reach its target unimpeded. Applications for other situations, such as the suppression of radar functions in a missile defense system, would potentially mitigate the need to fire a large amount of missiles to suppress a single target.

Cyber capabilities have also been used as isolated cases of strategic attacks. Examples such as Shamoon and DarkSeoul have shown that it is possible to disrupt an organization without physical infiltration or attack. Incidents such as Project Aurora and Stuxnet have shown that in some cases a cyber attack can physically destroy a target. This implies that if such capabilities are used in a sophisticated manner, it can reach a strategic target directly. Like early theories of strategic air bombing, malware with destructive functions may enable an attacker to bypass what John Warden called "concentric rings" and directly reach a desired target without mounting complex operations starting from the periphery. This may be particularly attractive for weaker entities, who cannot launch such a complex operation. Most importantly, it provides weaker military powers a more credible means to coerce a stronger adversary than the threat of conventional military power.

All this is even more attractive for the weaker military power especially if its own military and political apparatus do not rely on networks and cyber capabilities. If vulnerabilities are mutual and both sides have capabilities to exploit them, perhaps the two will seek ways to exercise a degree of mutual restraint. However, if vulnerabilities are asymmetric, where one side is heavily reliant on cyberspace for military, economic, and political activity while the other side barely uses them, the latter is less beholden to the prospect of losing such capabilities in retaliation. The latter may not even invest in cyber defense because being connected is not a critical function. In such cases, the former cannot respond simply by returning an eye for an eye, but must find alternative ways to respond, which may or may not be politically viable.

This imbalance is even more severe when considering that there are few accepted international norms on appropriate state responses or countermeasures to a cyber attack, adding confusion for policymakers. Although attribution techniques have gotten better recently, for most advanced attacks it is still difficult to investigate the origin of an attack. Even if success is achieved, it is difficult to tie the originator to a state. International law enforcement cooperation on this is better for cyber crime for other malicious activities it is ad hoc and politically influenced. Current international law has not come to agreement on fundamental issues such as what actions in cyberspace constitute various degrees of aggressive state bevaior (i.e., armed attack or use of force), what would be a legitimate and proportional response in each case, and what the rights and duties of third parties are. Under these conditions, the defender currently has a hard time communicating red lines and threats that indicate that certain actions in cyberspace will be consistently and undeniably returned with appropriate costs.

FINAL NOTES

For the weaker military powers that rely on asymmetric strategies to counter an adversary's conventional strength, the strategic use of cyber capabilities is an especially attractive option. Relatively cost-effective and low risk, cyber means can exploit a significant adversary vulnerability. They can be used as coercion or as part of a larger operation. In this context, the DPRK's investment in cyber capabilities is hardly surprising.

DPRK Cyber Strategy

The DPRK's cyber strategy mainly stems from its larger asymmetric strategy. The DPRK's main opponents, the United States and ROK, are militarily and economically superior. Any attempt to change the unfavorable status quo must be done below the threshold of open war, as the DPRK could not presumably survive such a conflict. Thus the DPRK invests in asymmetric capabilities that allows it to project power and coerce without necessarily inciting a conventional military standoff.

Within this overall asymmetric strategy, North Korea's cyber strategy is influenced by two older traditions: the disruption of opposing conventional operations and the peacetime use of disruptive provocations. These two traditions roughly align with the DPRK's use of information and electronic warfare elements and the peacetime utilization of special forces for coercion. These traditions are operational or strategic concepts that existed before cyber capabilities, but the DPRK's conceptualization of cyber capabilities seems to stem from or relate to these ideas.

These two concepts, as well as North Korea's cyber capabilities, are aligned with the KPA General Staff Department (GSD) and the RGB. The GSD is associated more with the tradition of disrupting the opponent's conventional operations, while the RGB is more associated with this peacetime coercive concept. Because the DPRK does not generally publish its own doctrine and strategy, the traditions and trends of DPRK organizations must be examined in order to establish a working concept of North Korean cyber strategy.

Actual DPRK military doctrine and strategy, though heavily theorized in government agencies as well as think tanks, are somewhat difficult to ascertain. Although scholars can glean something of the DPRK's political and military strategy through following DPRK domestic news or proceedings of Korean Worker's Party (KWP) meetings, definitive statements of the doctrine are not published. The few resources available outside the DPRK are typically classified.[38] Modern DPRK doctrine and strategy has origins in Soviet and PLA military training, evolving into its current form and tailored to the DPRK's unique needs.[39]

The DPRK's disruptive cyber capabilities are mainly under the control of the KPA GSD and RGB, with smaller intelligence functions possibly under the KWP. While other functions that take place in cyberspace, such as psychological warfare and propaganda, are also spread across different organizations including the RGB, GSD, and KWP, these are outside the scope of this report. Generally, the KPA's cyber units seem to have evolved from DPRK electronic warfare concepts, while the RGB's cyber units have roots in irregular and asymmetric operations including provocations, reconnaissance, and criminal activities. This is in accordance with the respective organizations' historic goals and missions. This dual

---

38. North Korea's "Electronic Warfare Reference Guide (전자전참고자료)," which was leaked in 2010, is an example.

39. James Minnich and Joseph Bermudez have conducted extensive research on DPRK's military doctrine, whose works are cited throughout this document. For further information, see Minnich, *North Korean People's Army*, and Joseph S. Bermudez, *North Korean Special Forces* (Annapolis, MD: Naval Institute Press, 1997).

tradition means that the different organizations conducting cyber operations may exercise cyber power in different ways and to meet different strategic or operational ends.

As will be further discussed in Chapter 2, the GSD's units are also partially theoretical. The RGB is the organization attributed with operations against the United States and ROK, while the GSD is not. Trends in DPRK strategy and statements made by DPRK leaders indicate that the GSD *should* follow a development path that involves significant cyber capabilities, but it is the RGB that currently is the dominant organization.

TRADITIONS IN PEACETIME PROVOCATIONS

The first tradition in the DPRK's military strategy relevant to our understanding of its cyber strategy is North Korea's reliance on irregular peacetime operations to sidestep the conventional deadlock on the Korean peninsula and coerce its opponents. Operation Orchard, Desert Storm, and other examples of traditional combat have started to show the value of joint military operations involving cyber capabilities, but these are not always applicable lessons for a tense peacetime environment. As such, more clandestine means are necessary to achieve national goals. The DPRK has conducted high-profile cyber operations against South Korean targets, broadly comparable to special operations in cyberspace. Even in peacetime, DPRK intelligence organizations and special forces are continuing their traditional missions, but seem to be augmenting or replacing more traditional capabilities with cyber capabilities for various reasons including convenience, secrecy, and cost.

As it became apparent that the DPRK could not conventionally overwhelm the ROK, the DPRK instead began to invest in asymmetric military capabilities for use outside of the conventional military realm.[40] These include the expansion of its special forces, investment in ballistic missile technologies, nuclear development, and, most recently, cyber capabilities. These capabilities not only allow for the potential improvement of the DPRK's position relative to the ROK during peacetime, but also serve as effective weapons during wartime.

As long as the Korean peninsula stays locked in a stalemate, especially with ROK and U.S. conventional superiority, and the DPRK still aims to undermine the ROK, the DPRK will be motivated to diversify its arsenal of asymmetric and unconventional weapons. The DPRK will find very valuable any capability that gives it the opportunity to defend itself from, diminish the advantages of, or otherwise harm the ROK without facing comparable retaliation. Essentially, these capabilities allow the DPRK to fight the United States and ROK without ever actually *fighting* the United States and ROK.

The DPRK has tried to assassinate two different ROK leaders, Park Chung-hee and Chun Doo-hwan, via high-profile commando raids on the Blue House in South Korea and a bombing at a memorial in Rangoon, respectively. In addition, the DPRK has a history of kidnapping both Japanese and Korean citizens for the purposes of information gathering and

---

40. Bruce E. Bechtol Jr., "Maintaining a Rogue Military: North Korea's Military Capabilities and Strategy at the End of the Kim Jong-Il Era," *International Journal of Korean Studies* 16, no. 1 (2012): 4, 163.

language and cultural training. It sank the *Cheonan*, destroyed a civilian airliner, and, at least as of the 1990s, was still sending midget submarines with special operations forces onboard around the ROK coast.[41] In addition, DPRK citizens and affiliates abroad have been repeatedly accused of generating funds and hard currency for the DPRK through illicit activities, such as narcotics sales and gambling.[42]

Many of these activities are linked with the DPRK's reconnaissance, intelligence, and special forces office, the RGB, or the historical units that were used to build the RGB. Most of the high-profile attacks associated with the DPRK are tied to the current or former offices and officers of the RGB.

The RGB is the current nexus and alleged main perpetrator of DPRK asymmetric provocations and cyber attacks. The RGB is made up of numerous offices and units formerly associated with provocative and offensive units from across the DPRK government structure, including elements pulled originally from the Korean Worker's Party itself. Whereas the GSD is mainly military and conventional war focused, the RGB functions as a combination intelligence organ and black/special operations force that can spy, abduct, and provoke during peacetime. It allows the DPRK to actively contest ROK's authority on the Korean peninsula without resorting to open violence.

Two of the most highly publicized asymmetric capabilities the DPRK maintains are nuclear and ballistic missile capabilities. While these are neither part of the Reconnaissance General Bureau nor within the scope of this assessment, they do help sum up the DPRK's asymmetric strategy fairly well. By pouring money into a few highly effective, highly threatening systems that target either a weak point of an opponent (i.e., civilian populations) or threaten to seriously increase the cost of war for an opponent (i.e., the huge cost of managing operations that have gone nuclear, cleanup, threat of destruction of ground formations), the DPRK makes the most of its strained budget. By picking choice systems that multiply the effectiveness of its own performance or seriously reduce the effectiveness of an opponent, either via threat/deterrence or actual use, the DPRK is making a theoretically wise investment.

While nuclear weapons are not particularly analogous to cyber warfare, the logic behind the investment is. Cyber warfare capabilities can be used to disrupt and destroy enemy information networks, and many developed states' militaries are now extensively networked and reliant on these networks. While the DPRK may not get its own force multiplier from cyber capabilities, it may get a "force de-multiplier" against the United States and ROK.

The DPRK may have concluded that its offensive cyber capabilities are as strategically important as its nuclear program. Kim Jong-un allegedly said, "Cyber warfare, along with nuclear weapons and missiles, is an 'all-purpose sword (만능의 보검)' that guarantees our

---

41. Bermudez, "New Emphasis."
42. Ibid.

military's capability to strike relentlessly," as revealed by Nam Jae-joon, director of South Korea's National Intelligence Service (NIS), in testimony at a National Assembly Intelligence Committee hearing in November 2013.[43] This statement is significant in that the DPRK may regard cyber capabilities as *strategic weapons,* as something more than just electronic jammers or a reconnaissance tool in a tactical setting. Cyber capabilities may have taken a central rather than supporting role in the DPRK's military strategy.

Much like nuclear and missile tests, cyber capabilities allow the DPRK to act around the deadlock on the peninsula and influence events in the ROK and United States. Cyber capabilities may have taken the place of the increasingly risky commando raids of the 1960s and 1970s. These capabilities allow for coercion with minimal operational risk, because there is no hardware or operatives that can be destroyed during the operation. However, public panic can be induced, financial systems can be disrupted, and illicit currency can still be generated.

TRADITIONS IN DISRUPTIVE CONVENTIONAL OPERATIONS

Part of the DPRK's drive for cyber warfare capabilities is a natural progression from its interest in engaging in information and electronic warfare to disrupt command and control in military operations. Even in the mid-1980s, concepts commonly referred to as "electronic information warfare" were developed at numerous research and educational institutions in the DPRK.[44] The U.S. military had superior electronic warfare capabilities and a growing dependence on sensor technologies and electronic communications networks. The DPRK saw the need to adapt to both defend its communications and disrupt U.S. and ROK communications and networks. U.S. electronic warfare and general electronic development was likely highlighted for DPRK planners when North Korean naval vessels captured the USS *Pueblo* in 1968 and examined the technology aboard. The *Pueblo* was used for communications and signals intelligence gathering. As computers and digital networking became obvious necessities for efficient command and control and logistics, they became obvious resources to pursue.

Historically, KPA military strategy and doctrine, as far as what has been studied in open sources, was originally conceived as a combination of those from the Soviet Union and the People's Republic of China. USSR concepts and theoretical frameworks for operational art, heavy mechanization, and the like mixed with PRC concepts of guerilla warfare and light infantry warfare to form the bedrock of DPRK doctrine and thought.[45] Although the DPRK has neither the same level of heavy army as the USSR nor the potential manpower of the PLA, elements from both states' doctrines were highly influential as both states had a major hand in training the Korean People's Army. As well, both the USSR and PRC had

---

43. Hyungsoo Kim, "Kim Jong-Un Says 'Cyber Warfare Is an All-Powerful Tool,' Utilizes It as One of Three Major Means of Warfare," *Joongang Ilbo,* November 5, 2013, http://nk.joins.com/news/view.asp?aid=12640100.

44. Joseph S. Bermudez, "SIGINT, EW, and EIW in the Korean People's Army: An Overview of Development and Organization," in *Bytes and Bullets: Information Technology Revolution and National Security on the Korean peninsula,* ed. Alexandre Y. Mansourov (Honolulu, HI: Asia-Pacific Center for Security Studies, 2005), 240–245.

45. Minnich, *North Korean People's Army.*

experience fighting and defeating well-armed and better funded opponents with strategically decisive results.

The DPRK learned from the Korean War that a protracted war against the United States is unfavorable and that it needs to adopt a strategy to win a quick, decisive war in the Korean peninsula. A quick, decisive war is attained by a surprise first strike that attacks from both the front and rear simultaneously, and an agile army that can strike at South Korea's center of gravity with speed and force. This would allow the DPRK to be in a favorable military and political situation before U.S. reinforcements could arrive, and possibly put the DPRK in a favorable position to earn further concessions through negotiations. For this to succeed, speed and accurate command and control is paramount for success, as is any possible attainable disruption in enemy logistics and information.[46]

One nontechnical example of the DPRK's drive for asymmetric advantage in wartime is within its light infantry corps.[47] Over the years, the DPRK has, at the expense of its standard infantry units, enlarged its light infantry units and emphasized the ability to wage irregular war on multiple fronts.[48] Light infantry, for the modern Korean People's Army, means highly mobile special purpose forces that wage irregular and asymmetric war. This means deploying to ROK rear areas and the targeted disruption of any possible military related system, in the hopes of inducing systemic collapse or the thinning of frontline forces. Instead of investing in the continued expansion of standard frontline infantry, the DPRK has invested in the enlargement of its light infantry forces to ensure its ability to wage irregular war.

Some of the most important strategic lessons relevant to DPRK cyber capabilities today, especially for the traditional military, come from the case of the Gulf War. The Iraq War is also of special significance. U.S. operations have likely taught the DPRK that the United States can have difficulty rallying domestic and international opinion, and that getting U.S. boots on the ground can be an arduous task,[49] but also that a highly advanced, networked army can be devastatingly effective against the conventional forces of an opposing state.

Kim Heung-kwang, a former Hamheung University of Computer Science professor who defected to the South in 2003, summarized DPRK's information warfare strategy as the securing of DPRK's command and control systems (called command automation in the DPRK) from enemy attack, ensuring access to the flow of information for achieving military objectives, and the destruction of enemy's capability to secure its systems. He states that the KPA is integrating information warfare capabilities into all branches of the military under the oversight of a centralized unit under the GSD, but with specific offensively

---

46. Kwon, *The Comprehension of North Korean Military*.
47. In this case, light infantry means nonmechanized footmobile infantry units that would wage irregular warfare and cause disruptions from within the ROK rear areas. It does not necessarily mean that they are poorly equipped or incapable of major military action.
48. Bermudez, "New Emphasis."
49. Minnich, *North Korean People's Army*.

oriented capabilities under the Air Force and various special forces units with an emphasis on joint operations.[50]

Kim's description is consistent with a military trying to integrate cyber capabilities into its main forces and trying to become a networked army with the dual missions of disrupting enemy networks while preserving its own. While he explicitly uses the phrase "information warfare," his descriptions also fall partially in the realm of cyber warfare and cyber capabilities. It is important to note that securing and disrupting systems, a function of cyber warfare, is thought of as a part of a larger information warfare strategy, which is more closely aligned with how PRC has conceptualized cyber warfare than how the United States has conceptualized it. One of the key differences between the two is that the main target to the secured or disputed is *information*, not cyberspace. Cyberspace is seen as one of many mediums though which a military transmits information. Other mediums can be anything from radio to written letters delivered by courier or a pigeon.

Operation Desert Storm was particularly influential for the DPRK's understanding of modern warfare and its decision to pursue cyber and other asymmetric options.[51] The military and the government devoted significant time to studying and understanding the coalition's successes in network and cyber based operations.[52] Defector testimony indicates that videotapes of U.S. operations in the Gulf War were repeatedly watched by military officers to better understand U.S. modern tactics, operations, and strategy.[53] According to Kim Heung-kwang, the DPRK realized the importance of electronic warfare in modern wars, and established the Automation Department under the GSD as well as electronic warfare research labs under each armed service to ensure DPRK's command and control capabilities as well as to disrupt that of an adversary.[54] Both the Gulf War and more recent Iraq War demonstrated to the DPRK the success of networked armies in war.[55]

Through analyzing North Atlantic Treaty Organization (NATO) campaigns during the 1999 Kosovo War, DPRK leadership again identified deficient C4ISR capabilities as a significant military disadvantage. The DPRK actively revised its strategy. Realizing that military use of the Internet and high-speed networks have significant implications for military operations, the DPRK created relevant technical departments in major war colleges.[56] The DPRK's military leadership also closely monitored the 2003 Iraq War via CNN and realized the central role of effective C4ISR in modern warfare. Allegedly, Kim Jong-il convened a high-level meeting after the Iraq War and asserted, "If warfare was about bullets and oil until now, warfare in the 21st century is about information. War is won and lost by who has greater access to the adversary's military technical information in peacetime, how

---

50. Kim, "Responses and Strategies."
51. Joseph S. Bermudez, "Command and Control," in *The Armed Forces of North Korea* (London: I. B. Tauris, 2001), 36; Kuehl, "From Cyberspace to Cyberpower."
52. Bermudez, "Command and Control," 242–244.
53. Joseph S. Bermudez, "North Korea's Strategic Culture" (Washington, DC: Defense Threat Reduction Agency, 2006).
54. Kim, "Responses and Strategies."
55. Ibid.
56. Ibid.

effectively one can disrupt the adversary's military command and control information, and how effectively one can utilize one's own information."[57] In the DPRK's classified *Electronic Warfare Reference Guide,* Kim Jong-il is also quoted as having said that "modern warfare is electronic warfare. The modern war is decided by one's conduct of electronic warfare."[58]

Beyond this point, it is difficult to ascertain whether the DPRK's cyber warfare strategy developed only as a continuation of the DPRK's information and electronic warfare strategy, or whether it diverged from these at a certain point. One important observation, however, is that the DPRK has paid very close attention to how major wars around the world have been fought. It has actively incorporated lessons from these wars into its own military strategy. The DPRK may be politically and economically isolated, but it would be a mistake to assume that the top leadership and the military are equally isolated from the military trends of modern warfare.

It is also worth noting that the theoretical concepts for cyber capabilities and electronic warfare being extensions of a larger information warfare concept exists in PLA writings as well. Instead of conceptualizing EW and cyber capabilities as domains or elements of a larger electromagnetic-spectrum domain, it can be conceptualized as the movement, protection, disruption, and falsification of information and data. This can tie it, somewhat confusingly, into other notions of intelligence, counterintelligence, and the like. This is not to say that the KPA and PLA share or shared EW and cyber doctrine, though that is a possibility. These notions also may stem from older Soviet concepts involving information warfare and political narrative control during warfare.

One of the possible ways that the DPRK has developed its cyber warfare strategy might be a combination of its information and electronic warfare strategy, combined with its long-standing strategy of fighting a blitzkrieg-style war on the Korean peninsula. A series of cyber attacks in the initial stages of war could achieve multiple effects. Like Operation Orchard, it could disrupt or destroy the radars and sensors necessary for missile or air defense. Like the 2008 Russo-Georgia War, DPRK could introduce chaos and hinder decisionmaking in the initial stages of conflict through widespread DDoS attacks or the use of wiper tools against vitial communication functions. The goal, much like jammers for radio communications, would be to disrupt U.S.-ROK active utilization of cyberspace for military purposes, thereby slowing down command and control.

In a much more literal comparison to Nazi Germany's blitzkrieg, instead of having a series of infantry engagements at the front of the operational area that act effectively as distractions to prevent the main armored force from being impeded, cyber capabilities act as an isolating and distracting force. The main equivalent of the armored thrust is screened and protected by a breakdown in U.S. and ROK C4ISR, and inefficiencies lead to operational or even strategic encirclement of targets. This is an ideal scenario for the DPRK.

---

57. Ibid.
58. Cited in Yong-hyun Ahn, "North Korea's Electronic Warfare Capability," *Chosun Ilbo,* March 7, 2011, http://news.chosun.com/site/data/html_dir/2011/03/07/2011030702345.html.

Possible DPRK Cyber Operations in Peacetime and Conflict

	Main DPRK Organization	Asymmetric Strategy	Historical Irregular Operations	Examples of Cyber Operations (Current)	Examples of Cyber Operations (Hypothetical)
Peacetime	RGB	Upset status quo via provocations	Blue House Raid, sinking of the *Cheonan*	Disruption of ROK banking, Sony attack	
Conflict	GSD/KPA	Disrupt enemy operations	Jammed ROK AN/TPQ-37 radar before artillery fire on Yeonpyeong Island Nov. 2010 (possibly joint operation with RGB)		Disrupting radar networks and early warning systems

Note: DPRK, Democratic People's Republic of Korea (North Korea); GSD, General Staff Department; KPA, Korean People's Army; RGB, Reconnaissance General Bureau; ROK, Republic of Korea (South Korea).

The end effect might be that the DPRK's decision cycles may be faster than the United States or ROK, at least in the initial stages of war, allowing it to exploit U.S. and ROK weaknesses and engage in maneuver warfare before the conflict can turn attritive. The danger of this possible development is not that the DPRK will actually execute this and successfully win a war on the Korean peninsula, but the DPRK miscalculates based on an overconfident notion of its own asymmetric strength.

The DPRK's strategic history has shown a pursuit of capabilities that can upset a stronger enemy. For the DPRK, its main opponents—the United States and ROK—have modern, network-dependent forces. In the same way that electronic warfare is vital for disrupting an army that depends heavily on sensor technologies, disruptive cyber operations seem vital for disrupting an army dependent on computer technologies.

FINAL NOTES

The DPRK's development of cyber capabilities is the result of a deliberate and careful assessment of its own strategic position and evolving trends in international conflict. It is the continuation of the DPRK's asymmetric strategy, and specifically influenced by concepts of disruptive conventional operations and peacetime irregular operations. The DPRK likely has a clear understanding of how cyber capabilities can serve its strategic objectives.

The DPRK views cyber capabilities as its answer to a flexible, networked adversary that enjoys near-real time battlefield data among its forces. From the KPA's vantage point, catching up with the modern military is probably not feasible, but falling too far behind is not acceptable either. If the KPA cannot conventionally match the technologically advanced weaponry of the United States and ROK, the next best thing is to disrupt the very technology that those weapons systems employ. This chapter's theoretical analysis is based on previous DPRK behavior with similar technologies and capabilities in addition to DPRK strategy and operational concepts.

Cyber capabilities offer a new and less risky option for crime, provocations, and sabotage when compared with the commando infiltrations and assassinations that were pervasive during the Cold War. In this context, it is hardly surprising that RGB is the main organization that houses the DPRK's cyber capabilities, in which it applies the same framework that it utilized commandos and special operatives for conventional provocations. Cyber capabilities may not be the key to military victory, but they do seem to offer a means of upsetting North Korea's opponents in peacetime.

2 | Organization

This chapter focuses on the organizations and support structure for North Korea's cyber capabilities and the units that control those capabilities. It will establish a base context for how cyber units are organized and the general chain of command as it is currently known. This is vital for predicting the general uses, goals, and missions of the various cyber components of the North Korean security apparatus.

In contrast to conventional warfighting capabilities, gauging a country's cyber capabilities is significantly challenging, given that the weapons employed in cyber warfare are elusive. Despite the difficulties, constant attempts have been made to quantify North Korea's cyber warfare capabilities, as shown in the South Korean government's 2015 estimate of 6,800 North Korean hackers.[1] Such numbers, if true, may provide North Korea watchers a glimpse of where they are at now. However, the sophistication of the organizations that conduct the regime's cyber operations and the technological base that buttresses their activities serves as better a indicator of the long-term outlook of North Korea's cyber capabilities.

Reconnaissance General Bureau

This section will outline the DPRK's Reconnaissance General Bureau (RGB) (정찰총국), thought to be the center of North Korean cyber activity as well as more traditional terrorist and clandestine activity. Understanding the RGB's organizational history, lineage, and internal organization illuminates *how* the DPRK utilizes and conceptualizes cyber capabilities. The RGB's association with cyber activity as well as with terrorist, clandestine, and illicit activities indicates that the DPRK likely sees cyber capabilities as powerful clandestine tools for national action.

Around 2009 and 2010, the DPRK restructured some of its intelligence organs, which altered the organization of their cyber warfare assets and moved a large number of units associated with cyber attacks and espionage under one roof. Units spread between the Korean Worker's Party (KWP) and the Ministry of People's Armed Forces (MPAF) were combined into the RGB, which also included a number of special forces and espionage-related units.

---

1. Seok-min Oh, "N. Korea Boosts Cyber Operations Capabilities," Yonhap News Agency, May 10, 2015, http://english.yonhapnews.co.kr/news/2015/05/08/97/0200000000AEN20150508006900315F.html.

The RGB is a hub of North Korean intelligence, commando, and sabotage operations. The RGB history of its leadership and component parts paints a picture of a one-stop shop for illegal and clandestine activity conducted outside the DPRK. The RGB and, prior to 2009 its component parts, have been involved in everything from maritime-inserted commando raids to abductions and spying. For the RGB to be in control of cyber assets indicates that the DPRK intends to use these assets for provocative purposes.

BACKGROUND OF THE RGB

The RGB is the linchpin of the DPRK's cyber operations, as well as its clandestine operations. The RGB is a relatively new organization, formed in 2009 from a large-scale reorganization of various existing offices and departments from across the North Korean government structure. These units were associated with a wide range of activities including political warfare, foreign intelligence collection, subversion, kidnapping, special operations, and assassinations. Major conventional provocations against South Korea such as the 1968 Blue House Raid, the 1983 Rangoon bombing, and the 2010 sinking of the *Cheonan* have been attributed to the RGB or one of its predecessor organizations such as the MPAF Reconnaissance Bureau.[2] More recently, the South Korean Ministry of National Defense reported that an RGB operative posing as a defector was arrested in March 2013.[3] The RGB's mission is not readily comparable or analogous to any organization in the U.S. government. It is best described as a hybrid organization encompassing aspects of statecraft, excluding conventional warfare, that include intelligence, illicit trade, commando operations, special/irregular operations, and cyber operations.

When the U.S. or South Korean government attributes a cyber operation to a specific North Korean organization, it is either the RGB itself or an RGB subunit that is named. The RGB is the current main organization responsible for the DPRK's cyber operations, including research, intelligence collection, and operations according to open-source data. While the Korean People's Army (KPA) does maintain cyber capabilities, it is the RGB that is reported to be the most active. The RGB's component organizations have a history of engaging in terrorism, espionage, as well as illicit arms trade. The RGB's association with cyber capabilities indicates that leadership within the DPRK sees cyber capabilities as tools for continuing provocations and possibly as complements to existing intelligence, terrorist, and black operations units.

LEADERSHIP

General Kim Yong-chol has been the director of the RGB since its formation in 2009.[4] He was previously the deputy director of the MPAF Reconnaissance Bureau, which has been

---

2. Bermudez, "New Emphasis."
3. ROK Ministry of National Defense, "2014 Defense White Paper" (Seoul, South Korea, 2014), http://www .mnd.go.kr/user/mnd/upload/pblictn/PBLICTNEBOOK_201506120237036840.pdf, 276.
4. ROK Ministry of Unification, "Profile: Kim Yong-chol," North Korea Information Portal, accessed November 17, 2015, http://nkinfo.unikorea.go.kr/nkp/theme/viewPeople.do?nkpmno=945.

now merged into the RGB,[5] possibly as the 2nd Bureau. The MPAF Reconnaissance Bureau was known for having planned and executed numerous provocations and commando operations. General Kim is a graduate of the Mangyongdae Revolutionary School and Kim Il-sung Military University, and served as a DPRK representative for a number of inter-Korean talks from 1989 to 2006.[6] He is believed to have been closely involved with the sinking of the *Cheonan* in 2010. Kim Yong-chol enjoys close ties with the Kim presidential family. Since serving as director of the RGB he was elected to be a member of the KWP and the Central Military Commission during the 3rd Party Conference in September 2010.[7] He was appointed as a four-star general in February 2012. After a brief demotion to lieutenant general in November 2012, he was again promoted to general in February 2013.[8] General Kim met with General James Clapper, U.S. director of national intelligence (DNI), in 2014, ostensibly in regards to the release of American citizens held in North Korea.[9] General Kim indicated during this meeting that he was the North Korean organizational equivalent of DNI Clapper.[10]

It is not clear whether Kim Yong-chol reports directly to Kim Jong-un given his close ties with him, or whether he works through the formal reporting channel through General O Kuk-ryol, who has overseen foreign intelligence and special operations as vice chairman of the National Defense Commission (NDC) since February 2009.[11] Although South Korean media, reporting the formation of the RGB, stated that O Kuk-ryol oversees the RGB, there is a possibility that this formal relationship has since faded.[12]

O Kuk-ryol has been one of the most important military figures in the DPRK. Born in 1931 in Jilin Province, General O was raised by Kim Il-sung's first wife, and his family has had very close ties with the Kim family. After graduating the Mangyongdae Revolutionary

5. "Gen. Kim Yong Chol," North Korea Leadership Watch, https://nkleadershipwatch.wordpress.com/leadership-biographies/lt-gen-kim-yong-chol/.

6. ROK Ministry of Unification, "Profile: Kim Yong-chol."

7. "Gen. Kim Yong Chol."

8. ROK Ministry of Unification, "Profile: Kim Yong-chol."

9. Nate Thayer, "American Spy Chief Secret Meeting with Head of North Korean Cyber Warfare," Nate Thayer–Journalist, January 9, 2015, http://www.nate-thayer.com/american-spy-chief-secret-meeting-with-head-of-north-korean-cyber-warfare/.

10. James R. Clapper, "Remarks as Delivered by DNI James R. Clapper on 'National Intelligence, North Korea, and the National Cyber Discussion' at the International Conference on Cyber Security," Fordham University, January 7, 2015), http://www.dni.gov/index.php/newsroom/speeches-and-interviews/208-speeches-interviews-2015/1156-remarks-as-delivered-by-dni-james-r-clapper-on-%E2%80%9Cnational-intelligence,-north-korea,-and-the-national-cyber-discussion%E2%80%9D-at-the-international-conference-on-cyber-security.

11. Min Namgoong, "North Korea's Reconnaissance Bureau Is a Direct Subordinate Organization under the National Defence Commission," *DailyNK*, April 21, 2010, http://www.dailynk.com/korean/read.php?cataId=nk01500&num=82869; ROK Ministry of Unification, "Profile: O Kuk-ryol," North Korea Information Portal, accessed November 17, 2015, http://nkinfo.unikorea.go.kr/nkp/theme/viewPeople.do?nkpmno=1072; "Gen. Kim Yong Chol."

12. Namgoong, "North Korea's Reconnaissance Bureau"; Sunyoung Choi, "North Korea's Sabotage Organizations against South Korea Merged as General Reconnaissance Bureau," *Yonhap News*, May 10, 2009, http://www.yonhapnews.co.kr/politics/2009/05/09/0521000000AKR20090509041100014.HTML; Bumjin Lee, "If North Korea Was behind Cheonan Sinking, General Reconnaissance Bureau's Kim Yong-Chol Likely to Have Led the Operation . . . Kim Kyuk-Sik of the Fourth Corps Also Plausible," *Chosun Weekly*, May 3, 2010, http://weekly.chosun.com/client/news/viw.asp?ctcd=C01&nNewsNumb=002103100000.

School and Kim Il-sung University, he received further military education at Frunze Military Academy in the Soviet Union in 1962. He then served in a number of important military and political positions, including KPA chief of the General Staff Department in 1979 and member of the KWP Politburo and the Central Military Committee.[13] After a brief demotion in 1988, he returned to power and became the director of the KWP Operations Department in 1989,[14] a position he held for nearly 20 years, lasting until the unit was merged into the RGB, possibly as the 1st Bureau. With the reshuffle, General O was appointed vice chairman of the NDC in February 2009. He has been deeply involved with the DPRK's intelligence operations as director of the KWP Operations Department, which primarily was responsible for infiltration, commando operations, and human intelligence in the ROK and foreign countries. General O is also said to have led the effort in establishing the Mirim College (now Kim-il Military Academy) in 1986 to raise a new cadre of officers focusing on electronic warfare as the then new Electronic Warfare Bureau was created under the General Staff Department (GSD).[15]

ORGANIZATION

The RGB, at least formally, directly reports to the National Defense Commission.[16] As stated previously, it is unclear to what degree the NDC actually supervises operations and activities of the RGB. Particularly important are rumors that upper leadership, including Kim Jong-un and O Kuk-ryol, are directly involved with the guidance of Bureau 121, the major cyber element of the RGB. These rumors are currently unsubstantiated, but seem logical because the cyber operations and provocations may be seen as matters of very high importance for DPRK leadership. Like all DPRK institutions, the organization of the RGB is opaque. However, open sources point to it having at least seven bureaus now, the six bureaus reported in 2010[17] and 2013[18] and a new seventh bureau known as Bureau 121. The first six bureaus are Operations, Reconnaissance, Foreign Intelligence, Inter-Korean Dialogue, Technical, and Rear Services, respectively.[19]

These bureaus came from the offices and units brought together during the 2009 reorganization. It is not fully known what the responsibilities of each bureau of the RGB are. It is entirely possible that the aforementioned names and descriptions used for each bureau, which are taken usually from their previous unit or office name, are not fully representative of current duties. The names may be legacies held over from previous responsibilities.

---

13. ROK Ministry of Unification, "Profile: O Kuk-ryol."

14. Sung-ha Joo, "The Fate of the O Kuk Ryol Family," *Pyongyang Story Written in Seoul*, January 29, 2014, http://blog.donga.com/nambukstory/archives/76397; Bermudez, "New Emphasis."

15. "Mirim College: Establishment and Current Activity," *NK Chosun*, October 31, 2013, http://nk.chosun.com/bbs/list.html?table=bbs_29&idxno=4282&page=2&total=112&sc_area=&sc_word=.

16. Ibid.; Bermudez, "New Emphasis."

17. Bermudez, "New Emphasis."

18. U.S. Department of Defense, *Military and Security Developments Involving the Democratic People's Republic of Korea 2013* (Washington, DC, 2013), http://www.defense.gov/pubs/North_Korea_Military_Power_Report_2013-2014.pdf.

19. Bermudez, "New Emphasis"; U.S. Department of Defense, *Military and Security Developments*.

Reconnaissance General Bureau Organization

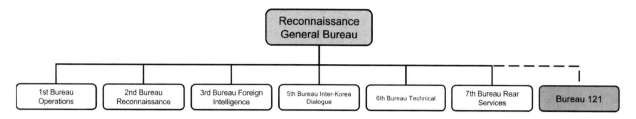

Source: Based partially on Joseph S. Bermudez Jr., "A New Emphasis on Operations Against South Korea?," 38 North Special Report, U.S. Korea Institute at School of Advanced International Studies (SAIS), 2010, http://38north.org/wp -content/uploads/2010/06/38north_SR_Bermudez2.pdf.

The RGB also operates a number of trading companies for arms trade, revenue generation, and technical acquisition. Of these companies, Green Pine Associate Corporation has been identified and sanctioned since 2012 pursuant to UN Security Council Resolution 1718 (2006) and by individual countries.[20]

HISTORY OF THE RGB

Mention of the RGB first appeared around 2009. Analyst Joseph Bermudez describes this new department as a centralized disruptive intelligence organization built out of numerous special operations and intelligence units previously under several different parts of the DPRK government.[21] The RGB is made up of a number of intelligence and special operations offices from the KWP and MPAF. The 1st, 2nd, and 3rd Bureaus reportedly have been formed from the KWP Operations Bureau, MPAF Reconnaissance Bureau, and KWP Office 35, respectively.[22] The 6th Bureau reportedly comes from the Radio/Technical unit from the MPAF Reconnaissance Bureau.[23] There is no specific indication that the 5th and 7th Bureaus, Inter-Korean Talks and Rear Services respectively, were created from other entities from across the DPRK government. It is unknown if they come from the original MPAF Reconnaissance Bureau, as the 6th Bureau did, or are new.

The KWP Operations Bureau, MPAF Reconnaissance Bureau, and KWP Office 35 have all been separately involved in intelligence and commando operations in South Korea and abroad. The MPAF Reconnaissance Bureau's main mission was collecting intelligence and the organization and command of several special operations units,[24] including the unit that perpetrated the Blue House Raid in 1968[25] and several other high-profile political and terrorist attacks. The KWP Operations Bureau and KWP Office 35 are described as playing a "central role in abductions, covert actions, and espionage as well as serving as elite

---

20. United Nations Security Council, "Security Council Committee Determines Entities, Goods Subject to Measures Imposed on Democratic People's Republic of Korea by Resolution 1718 (2006)," UN Press Release, May 2, 2012, http://www.un.org/press/en/2012/sc10633.doc.htm.
21. Bermudez, "New Emphasis."
22. Ibid.
23. Joseph S. Bermudez, interview with author, January 23, 2015, Allsource Analysis, Longmont, Colorado.
24. Robert L. Worden, *North Korea: A Country Study*, Library of Congress Federal Research Division (Washington, DC: GPO, 2008), http://archive.org/details/northkoreacountr00word, 250.
25. Bermudez, "New Emphasis."

bodyguards" and serving as "the main intelligence service," respectively.[26] The Radio/Technical unit from the MPAF Reconnaissance Bureau, which became the 6th Bureau, reportedly coordinated with the Electronic Warfare Bureau and Communications Bureau of the Korean People's Army General Staff Department.[27]

Since the initial reporting regarding the formation of the RGB in 2009, there is very little information regarding how the organization has expanded or been reorganized. The original bureaus may also have been modified, reorganized, or disbanded and no longer resemble the operations of their legacy organizations.

Until 2009 and 2010, the DPRK's general cyber capabilities were strewn about numerous departments, bureaus, and offices. For example, the MPAF Reconnaissance Bureau, KWP Operations Bureau,[28] KPA General Staff Department Electronic Warfare Bureau,[29] and unnamed elements of the State Security Department[30] all had missions or subordinate units with missions that likely involved network or cyber capabilities. Some of these were more reconnaissance, espionage, and possibly crime oriented, comparable to the Reconnaissance Bureau, while some were likely more disruption and warfare oriented, like the General Staff Department's Electronic Warfare Bureau. The 2009 reorganization brought much of the DPRK's known disruptive cyber capabilities under the control of the RGB, although the General Staff Department of the Korean People's Army did retain control of some military cyber capabilities.

It should be noted that as the DPRK gains operational experience and refines its cyber warfare doctrines, it would not be surprising for a few more major restructurings to occur. The United States, despite having cyber capabilities for years, did not form Cyber Command until the late 2000s, leaving cyber capabilities strewn about various offices, including the National Security Agency (NSA) and parts of the U.S. Air Force. The capabilities and structuring of cyber elements are tested and refined constantly, with new administration and organization emerging as a result.

CYBER UNITS OF THE RGB

This section will provide an overview of the specific units allegedly involved with the RGB's cyber operations as reported in open-source literature. Considerable uncertainty surrounds these units' origin, evolution, and mission. It is difficult to trace whether these units have been already integrated at some point in the past into a centralized, overarching bureau or whether these units still exist separately in distinct units. Some cyber units also seem to have alternate names or cover designations, a common feature in North Korea's deception and concealment efforts. Independent verification of these cyber units' existence

---

26. U.S. Senate Committee on Homeland Security and Governmental Affairs, *North Korea: Illicit Activity Funding the Regime*, 109th Cong., 2nd sess. (April 25, 2006), 68.
27. Bermudez, "SIGINT, EW, and EIW," 251.
28. Bermudez, "New Emphasis."
29. Bermudez, "SIGINT, EW, and EIW," 251.
30. Ibid., 235.

and operations is extremely difficult at the unclassified level. RGB units that are not primarily associated with cyber operations in open-source literature are not discussed. The bureaus, as well as the details about them, should be considered tentative information that requires further corroboration and verification.

Bureau 121 (Electronic Reconnaissance Bureau's Cyber Warfare Guidance Bureau [사이버전지도국])

Bureau 121 is the DPRK's most important cyber unit. Its wide range of cyberspace missions includes offensive and defensive cyber operations, cyber espionage, network exploitation, and cyber crime. Different sources refer to it by different names, including Unit 121, Bureau 121 (121국), and, the Electronic Reconnaissance Bureau's Cyber Warfare Guidance Bureau (전자정찰국 사이버전지도국). No report exists on who leads Bureau 121, although Kim Yong-chol, RGB's director, is reported to have a heavy hand in overseeing Bureau 121 activities, such as reports that he personally ordered an offensive cyber operation against Sony Pictures Entertainment.[31] North Korea Intellectuals Solidarity (NKIS), a North Korean defector organization, alleged that new headquarters were built in May 2013 for an expanded Bureau 121 in Uh-eun Dong, Ryongsong District in northern Pyongyang, located along with several luxury apartment complexes built for employees of Bureau 121.[32] Initial analysis of satellite imagery does not support this claim. However, if operations or facilities are underground, as is common within the DPRK, it would make it nearly impossible to identify via satellite imagery.

Bureau 121 is also reported in South Korean open-source media as having an alternative name, the Cyber Warfare Guidance Bureau under the Electronic Reconnaissance Bureau.[33] The DPRK's use of alternative names for major political and military organizations is not an uncommon phenomenon, and is often used as part of the state's denial and deception operations. If the above reports are true, then the fact that Bureau 121 is considered a guidance bureau is organizationally significant, because the term *guidance bureau* often denotes that an organization is personally overseen by the supreme commander and indicates that the leadership considers the unit strategically significant.[34]

---

31. "The Head of North Korea's General Reconnaissance Bureau Kim Yong-Chol Directly Ordered Sony Hacking," *MK News*, March 8, 2015, http://news.mk.co.kr/newsRead.php?year=2015&no=220454&utm_source =facebook&utm_medium=sns&utm_campaign=share.

32. "North Korea's Hacking Unit Elevated from Battalion to Brigade-Level through Reinforcement," North Korea Intellectuals Solidarity, August 8, 2013, http://www.nkis.kr/board.php?board=nkisb201&page=5 &command=body&no=472; "North Korea Newly Establishes Game Sabotage Unit in General Reconnaissance Bureau's Bureau 121, Deployed to Gather Foreign Currency," North Korea Intellectuals Solidarity, August 8, 2013, http://www.nkis.kr/board.php?board=nkisb201&command=body&no=533.

33. Jong-in Lim, "Major Countries around the World Are Preparing for Cyber Warfare Aggressively," *Science and Technology* 528, no. 5 (2013), http://www.kofst.or.kr/kofst/PDF/2013/n5s528/GGDCBE_2013_n5s528 _52.pdf.

34. Young-jong Lee, "Cyber Warfare Is KPA's 'Ruthless Sword,'" *Joongang Ilbo*, December 30, 2014, http:// www.sisapress.com/news/articleView.html?idxno=63782.

Computer Technology Research Lab (컴퓨터기술연구소)[35]

Very little has been reported about RGB's Computer Technology Research Lab. The last public reporting on this unit was in March 20, 2013, during a confirmation hearing for Nam Jae-joon, former NIS director, in which he identified this unit along with Lab No. 110 (110호 연구소)[36] as units possessing hacking techniques advanced enough to conduct destructive attacks on South Korean financial institutions.[37] It is unknown whether this unit continues to exist in this form or has been merged or disbanded, whether this unit is a cover designation for another RGB cyber unit, and where exactly this unit fits within RGB's larger organizational structure.

Nonetheless, the unit is worth mentioning due to one news article regarding operations of the Computer Technology Research Lab, because it is one of the few instances where a specific malware was linked with a developer at a North Korean cyber unit.[38] According to a July 2012 article by the New Focus, a South Korean Internet news outlet run by North Korean defectors, the Computer Technology Research Lab is directed by Colonel/Captain (상좌) Jo Myung-lae, graduate of Mirim College (now Kim-il Military College) and developer of what is called the "JML virus."[39] According to this source, Jo was born in 1964, graduated Mirim College in 1997 with a graduation thesis titled "The Militarization of Computer Viruses," and has subsequently worked as a graphic designer and in a research position at Korea Computer Center (KCC). He led a small computer research team at Mirim, which eventually became the current Computer Technology Research Lab under RGB. The source claimed that the lab is located behind KCNA (Korean Central News Agency) headquarters in Munsu-dong, Taedonggang District, Pyongyang.

---

35. The English nomenclature is the authors' direct translation of the organization's Korean name, and may have a slightly different official English name in the DPRK.

36. Details surrounding Lab No. 110 (110호 연구소) needs further research. The designation has circulated in open-source literature along with Unit 121 (Bureau 121's former designation). There is still considerable difficulty in tracing Lab No. 110's origins, missions, activity, and, most importantly, whether it has merged with Bureau 121. Lab No. 110 and Unit 121 have, in the past, been referred to as separate and distinct units, with Lab No. 110 being referred to in the South Korean media as a cyber warfare unit. However, the current missions of Bureau 121 seems to subsume this mission. Adding to the confusion is that some South Korean media sources refer to Lab No. 110 alternatively as Technical Reconnaissance Unit Lab No. 110 (기술정찰조 110호 연구소), but Unit 121 has also been alternatively named at some unidentified point in the past as the Technical Reconnaissance Unit (기술정찰조). In this regard, we have not been able to make a conclusive assessment on what the identity of Lab No. 110 is. It could be a current separate and distinct organ, a historical unit that has been incorporated into a larger unit, or simply a cover designation. This is an identified gap in research and merits further discussion.

37. Soonpyo Park, "North Korea Responsible for Most of 70,000 Cases of Cyberattacks during the Last Five Years," YTN, March 21, 2013, http://www.ytn.co.kr/_ln/0101_201303211024217337?ems=12714.

38. The authors' decision to mention this news article in our report should not be misconstrued as our endorsement regarding the validity of the contents of the news article. We have not been able to find ways to separately verify all contents of the article, but because it was one of the few instances in which a specific malware has been associated with a developer and his organization, we decided to mention it in our report so that other analysts could further confirm or deny its details.

39. Joon-sik Shin, "Information Regarding Jo Myung-Lae, Person in Charge of North Korea's Hacker Unit," *New Daily*, July 10, 2012, http://www.newdaily.co.kr/news/article.html?no=117038.

According to New Focus, Jo developed a malware called JML virus around 1997, which has since had many variants and was seen fairly frequently in the early 2000s.[40] Further research seems to indicate that Jo may have instead modified an existing malware named Win32/Weird. Because Win32/Weird was detected in 1999, there is a possibility that the date 1997 is incorrect unless Jo developed Win32/Weird himself and kept it for two years before releasing it in 1999. Research indicates that the official name of the so-called JML virus most likely refers to a malware that used to be called Win32/JML by AhnLab; the company changed the detection name to Win32/Weird.C in 2003.[41]

The original malware Win32/Weird[42] was discovered on July 6, 1999. It infects Windows and Windows system folders and has a back door. The original developer of the malware, who goes by the alias Weird and includes a "Coded by Weird" signature in his programs, subsequently revealed the source code of this malware online.[43] AhnLab claims that one variant of this original malware, Win32/Weird.B detected in 2002, was first reported in South Korea and has not been detected elsewhere at the time of the writing (neither Symantec nor McAfee have profiles on Win32/Weird.B).[44] If Jo and his team indeed developed and executed variants of this malware, it indicates that North Korean hackers did not develop their tools and techniques in isolation. Perhaps they had privileged access to the Internet and outside resources. No further open-source information has been found regarding what malware Jo or Computer Technology Research Lab developed, and whether any of the malware used in cyber attacks from the DPRK have been developed by this team.

1st Operations Bureau (작전국) 414 Liaison Office and 128 Liaison Office (414 연락소, 128 연락소)

South Korean media and research reports often cite the 414 Liaison Office and 128 Liaison Office (414, 128 연락소) as a major cyber unit under RGB.[45] However, a description of their functions, at least in open source, seems to indicate that their mission scope is

---

40. Ibid.

41. The malware also had a variant by the name of Win32/JML.29696, which was also changed to Win32/Weird.29696. "Periodical Engine Update—April 9, 2003," V3 MSS AhnLab, April 9, 2003, http://v3mss.ahnlab.com/front/board/update_view.do?nowPage=363&board.num=139381. Win32/Weird.C seems to have many aliases, further described in "Virus Profile: W32/Kuang.gen!1BB55FA83B30," McAfee, March 19, 2013, http://home.mcafee.com/virusinfo/virusprofile.aspx?key=2351728#none.

42. This malware has several aliases depending on the company that detected the virus, including Win95. Weird, Backdoor.Win32.KUANG2.10240, W95/Kuang.gen, PE_WEIRD.10240, and Win32.Weird.10240. Further technical information is available from "W32.Weird Technical Details," Symantec, February 13, 2007, http://www.symantec.com/security_response/writeup.jsp?docid=2000-121515-2958-99&tabid=2.

43. "W32.Weird Technical Details."

44. Ibid.

45. Dong-ryul Yoo, *Cyberspace and National Security* (Seoul: Korean Institute for Liberal Democracy, 2012), 55; Seung-ho Cho, "North Korea Has Trained about 3,000 Hackers," *DongA Ilbo*, March 21, 2013, http://news.donga.com/rel/3/all/20130321/53855571/1; Jong-duk Park, "North Korea Ranks 3rd in Cyber Power, Maintains a 30,000 Cyber Army," *Daily Journal*, August 13, 2013, http://www.dailyjn.com/news/articleView.html?idxno=14568; Hwa-jong Lee, "North Korea's Reconnaissance General Bureau's Cyber Unit Match CIA's Capabilities," *Munhwa Ilbo*, March 21, 2013, http://www.etimes.net/Service/CreditBank_2008/ShellView.asp?ArticleID=2013032113540601558.

limited to supporting intelligence collection in South Korea using cyber espionage as one of many means for their mission assurance. The existence of 414 and 128 Liaison Offices predate RGB and the DPRK's widespread use of cyber capabilities as intelligence mission support units in General O's KWP Operations Department (now RGB 1st Operations Bureau). It is possible that these units increasingly rely on cyber means, given the low risk and cost involved, and that some of the tools and techniques developed in the process are shared with other RGB units for initial penetration. Yet it seems to be an overstatement to characterize either of these units as a major cyber operations unit at the level of Bureau 121.

The term *liaison office* usually denotes a specific function in DPRK, specifically responsible for escorting and communicating with any commando or special operations forces sent to infiltrate South Korea. From what is available in the open source, the 414 Liaison Office has been responsible for maintaining communications with espionage networks in South Korea including relaying missions and receiving reports, and conducts surveillance on South Korean law enforcement and security agencies.[46] While it is possible that, over time, they have decided to conduct surveillance more efficiently via hacking into computers of South Korean law enforcement and security agencies, these activities seem to be aimed at performing counterintelligence to ensure continued communication with their espionage networks rather than directly aimed at achieving political and military objectives using cyber capabilities. It is most likely that liaison office utilization of cyber means is limited to supporting original missions, and these offices are unlikely to be major cyber operations units. There remains a low possibility that the names—414 Liaison Office and 128 Liaison Office—are cover designations and that the missions are now not related to the actual functions of a liaison office.

FINAL NOTES

The RGB is a nexus of illicit and provocative activities. Its missions seem to largely based on illicit activity and waging irregular operations against South Korea. Its control of cyber capabilities means that the United States and ROK should expect continued provocations in cyberspace and continued cyber operations aimed at eroding the U.S. and ROK positions, as this would be a continuation of its traditional asymmetric and irregular missions by means in cyberspace. The RGB may be the dominant cyber operational entity within the DPRK government structure, which could be indicative that DPRK leadership sees RGB-type activities as the most efficient use of their cyber capabilities and resources.

More research is necessary to fully explore the range of activities the RGB is responsible for, including the depth and details of Bureau 121's current status and organizational makeup. A full or even nearly full organizational chart of the RGB does not exist in any literature and likely will require intelligence community data to fully realize.

---

46. Michael Lee, "North Korea's Intelligence Operations against South Korea," Chogabje.com, November 3, 2014, http://www.chogabje.com/board/column/view.asp?C_IDX=58208&C_CC=BC.

Organization of the Cyber-Related Units of the General Staff Department

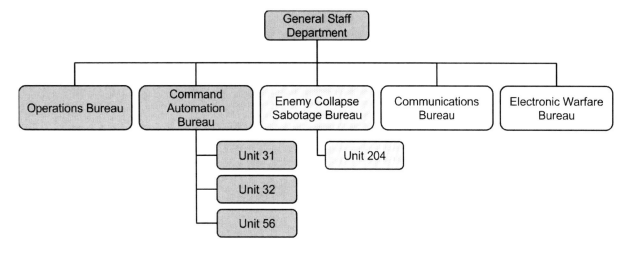

Note: Dark-shaded units are immediately relevant to cyber operations. Lighter-shaded units may include cyber capabilities that have missions outside the scope of this assessment. White is a partially related or a coordinating organization.

General Staff Department of the Korean People's Army

The GSD (총참모부), like most general staffs in other military organizations, is responsible for operational command as well as planning and management of the DPRK's military forces. Whereas the MPAF is typically associated more with politics and administration, the GSD is associated with operational planning. It reports directly to the NDC specifically to Kim Jong-un, the KPA supreme commander.[47] Although the MPAF is supposed to oversee the GSD according to bureaucratic design, the GSD is under the de facto direct control of the KPA supreme commander.[48] Allegedly, the MPAF's control over the GSD was strong when O Jin-woo, one of Kim Il-sung's closest aides, was leading the MPAF, but since then Kim Jong-il established direct control over the GSD and it has remained largely free from MPAF control.[49] Civilian oversight of the military is minimal in the DPRK.[50]

In addition to its more conventional oversight, the GSD oversees the general military aspects of the DPRK's cyber operations as well as other related missions such as electronic warfare, information warfare, and psychological operations. It has several subordinate organizations that, while having different general missions, work together and across other organizations such as the RGB to perform missions in and through cyberspace. Public information about the GSD's cyber units is less common than that of the RGB, which

---

47. "General Staff Department," North Korea Leadership Watch, January 16, 2011, https://nkleadershipwatch.wordpress.com/dprk-security-apparatus/general-staff-department/.

48. Kwon, *Comprehension of North Korean Military*.

49. Ibid.

50. Ken E. Gause, *North Korean Civil-Military Trends: Military-First Politics to a Point* (Carlisle, PA: Strategic Studies Institute, 2006).

has generated greater academic and policy attention after engaging in more high-profile cyber operations against civilian targets. What is known is that the GSD's cyber units have organizational roots in signal intelligence and electronic warfare from the early 1990s (see Chapter 1).

The GSD units relevant for an understanding of the DPRK's military cyber operations are the Operations Bureau, Communications Bureau, Electronic Warfare Bureau, the Command Automation Bureau, and the Enemy Collapse Sabotage Bureau. This assessment of the missions of GSD units relevant to cyber operations is based on what is reported in open-source media about their organization and an extrapolation of traditional missions.

OPERATIONS BUREAU (작전국)

The core mission of the Operations Bureau is operational military planning, strategy, and general management.[51] This means that the Operations Bureau, while not directly performing cyber operations, still may serve an important role in making key decisions related to cyber force planning, defining and disseminating cyber strategy, and deployment in particular missions. Most importantly, the DPRK's heavy emphasis on joint operations could be indicative of the Operations Bureau's involvement in integrating cyber operations into conventional military operations planning. Because of the high level of influence it has on the KPA, the Operations Bureau is an important organization within the GSD, with some experts assessing that there is a direct channel of communication between the supreme commander and the director of the Operations Bureau, at times bypassing the director of the GSD.[52] This direct channel could mean either that the Operations Bureau holds a particularly powerful and influential position within GSD or, because of its impact on the operation of the KPA, it is actually heavily micromanaged by Kim Jong-un in his role as supreme commander as a way to keep the military under control. The director of the Operations Bureau also has the title of first vice director of the GSD (제1부총참모장). KNCA reported on January 7, 2015, that Kim Chun-sam was appointed as the new director of the Operations Bureau.[53]

According to NKIS, the GSD held its first ever joint military exercise involving cyber command and control integration during a military-wide training exercise February 21–March 4, 2014.[54] Using the DPRK's Gold Star military network, which connects the GSD with commanders and soldiers, the GSD tested the military's electronic and information warfare capabilities. Allegedly, several researchers from the Kim-il Military College (former Mirim College) and Lab 78 under the RGB were commended for fixing problems with Gold Star and developing a command and control software for the training.[55] If true, this

---

51. "General Staff Department."
52. Gause, *North Korean Civil-Military Trends*, 18.
53. Gyung-rak Min, "Director of the Artillery Bureau of the General Staff, Who Played a Leading Role in the YP-Do Incident, Gets Promoted to General," *Yonhap News*, January 7, 2015, http://www.yonhapnews.co.kr /northkorea/2015/01/07/1801000000AKR20150107043300014.HTML.
54. "Kim Jong-Un's Instructions from March 8, 2014," North Korea Intellectuals Solidarity, May 29, 2014, http://www.nkis.kr/board.php?board=nkisb201&body_only=y&button_view=n&command=body&no=523.
55. Ibid.

indicates that DPRK may retain a consistent technical research and development (R&D) base for specific military missions and that aspects of electronic and cyber warfare are consciously integrated into the GSD's military planning. This also would indicate that there is a demand for cyber capabilities from the military, which may lead to greater institutional support including promotions, budget increases, and personnel allocation.

COMMAND AUTOMATION BUREAU (지휘자동화국)

The Command Automation Bureau reportedly conducts computer network operations (CNO) and has responsibility for developing malware and searching for exploits.[56] The bureau was established in the early 1990s after DPRK leadership, through analyzing the Gulf War, realized the importance of having a networked military and that cyber elements can present a vulnerability in an adversary's military that can be exploited.[57] Kim Heung-kwang describes the Command Automation Bureau as overseeing activities of the "reconnaissance units and the research labs" under the Army, Navy, and Air Force Commands, as well as the light infantry corps, although it is unclear as to what the duties of these "reconnaissance units and research labs" are.[58]

According to a 2009 report from the Korea Institute for National Unification, the Command Automation Bureau has around 50 to 60 officers in Unit 31, responsible for malware development; Unit 32, responsible for software development for military use; and Unit 56, responsible for developing military command and control software.[59] The report's description indicates that these units' primary mission is R&D, but also indicated that the units are routinely pulled in for specific missions. A 2014 NKIS report also mentioned that resources from Units 31, 32, and 56 were pulled into an RGB mission to exfiltrate information regarding warhead miniaturization and ballistic missile technology.[60]

ENEMY COLLAPSE SABOTAGE BUREAU (적군와해공작국 OR 적공국)[61]

South Korean popular media as well as experts such as Yoo Dong-yul often cite the Enemy Collapse Sabotage Bureau's Unit 204 as a cyber unit.[62] However, this unit is more properly characterized as a psychological or information warfare unit rather than a disruptive

---

56. "North Korea's Internal State of Affairs," *Korea Institute for National Unification's Monthly North Korea Review* 3, no. 4 (2009): 20.

57. Kim, "Responses and Strategies."

58. Ibid.

59. "North Korea's Internal State of Affairs."

60. "North Korea Employs All of Its Cyber Units Including Bureau 121 to Hack Information on Warhead Miniaturization and Ballistic Missile Technology," North Korea Intellectuals Solidarity, November 5, 2014, http://www.nkis.kr/board.php?board=nkisb201&command=body&no=553.

61. We placed this bureau as belonging under GSD in this report due to frequent association of this bureau to GSD by the popular media. However, as explained later in this section, this placement is disputed and may be actually placed under the General Political Bureau. The English translation of this organization's title is often inconsistent, and other scholars refer to this organization as either Enemy Attack Bureau or Enemy Collapse Bureau. See Alexandre Mansourov, "North Korea's Cyber Warfare and Challenges for the U.S.-ROK Alliance," KEI Academic Paper Series, Korea Economic Institute of America, December 2014, http://keia.org/sites/default/files/publications/kei_aps_mansourov_final.pdf.

62. Yoo, *Cyberspace and National Security.*

cyber unit. Unit 204's mission is described as using the Internet to spread anti-South Korean propaganda, but this falls outside of a typical definition of cyber operations if it is not actively stealing identities or compromising networks to plant false information. Unit 204, at most, would conduct CNE for propaganda and misinformation purposes, but it is hard to imagine that they would be conducting computer network attacks (CANs) or serve as an operational cyber warfare unit. The bureau as a whole, even before Unit 204 was created, seemed to focus primarily on propaganda. Without further evidence to prove otherwise, there is danger in conflating between psychological warfare and cyber warfare as it contributes to inflating North Korea's cyber threat.

However, because the media repeatedly mentions this organization, for purposes of context its functions are described below. The Enemy Collapse Sabotage Bureau reportedly is composed of three brigades each with around 600 to 700 personnel, for a total of 2,000. Although the bureau's relatively small size indicates that it should be headed by a division commander, it is reported to be headed by a lieutenant general or a general, indicating its heightened importance despite its size.[63] The bureau is also referred to as the 563th Army Unit.[64] The bureau's mission in peacetime is reported to be to recruit South Korean collaborators, spread propaganda, and prepare for infiltration to South Korea from third-party states; its wartime mission is to infiltrate as a paramilitary unit disguised as the South Korean military to disrupt their operations.[65]

Sources disagree on where this bureau falls in the DPRK's organizational structure; some say it is a bureau under the GSD while others claim it is under the General Political Bureau (총정치국), a powerful organization that exerts the KWP's ideological control over the military. Experts claim that the General Political Bureau is nominally under the MPAF but de facto controlled by the KWP's Organization and Guidance Department.[66] An organization that conducts similar missions against South Korea, the Propaganda and Agitation Department (선전선동부), is also under the General Political Bureau. In a November 2013 hearing at the National Assembly, the director of the NIS considered the Enemy Collapse Sabotage Bureau and the Propaganda and Agitation Department as two separate, distinct organizations.[67] While it was reported that this bureau was transferred from KPA control to the General Political Bureau in May 1965,[68] there is no further evidence in open sources as to whether this remained unchanged or whether the bureau was transferred to another

---

63. Sang-yong Lee, "Members of the Enemy Collapse Bureau, who Infiltrates South Korea on Backpacks, Meets Kim Jong-Un," *DailyNK*, November 12, 2013, http://www.dailynk.com/korean/read.php?cataId=nk00700&num=101611.

64. Jung-hoon Lee, "Kyung-Hak Jung, the First North Korean Spy Caught during the Roh Administration," *New DongA*, October 1, 2006, http://shindonga.donga.com/docs/magazine/shin/2006/10/13/200610130500016/200610130500016_1.html.

65. In-soo Choi, "Jae-Joon Nam, the Head of National Intelligence Service, Opposes Handing over Anti-Communist Investigation but Instead Gives a Detailed Report on North Korea's Cyber Psychological Warfare," *Joongang Ilbo*, November 4, 2013, http://article.joins.com/news/article/article.asp?Total_Id=13047219.

66. Bermudez, *Armed Forces of North Korea*, 28.

67. Choi, "Jae-Joon Nam."

68. Lee, "Kyung-Hak Jung."

organization such as the GSD.[69] The current association of the bureau with the GSD seems to stem from a statement from Kim Heung-kwang who said that North Korea created Unit 204 of the Enemy Collapse Sabotage Bureau in 1995 under the GSD, but it is unclear as to whether he is pointing to the creation of Unit 204 or the bureau itself.[70]

COMMUNICATIONS BUREAU (통신국)

The Communications Bureau overseas all administration and operations regarding communications within the KPA, including monitoring of domestic and foreign telecommunications and securing KPA communications.[71] Little new information is reported about this organization. According to Joseph Bermudez, the Communications Bureau worked closely with the State Security Department and the now reorganized Reconnaissance Bureau (moved as a subordinate unit of the RGB) in signals intelligence operations and also worked with the Classified Information Bureau, mainly responsible for encryption/decryption.[72] It seems that the duties of the Communications Bureau are in whole or in part comparable to that of the U.S. Army Signal Corps. At least one communications battalion, located in Pyongsong, is reported to be subordinate to the Communications Bureau, however no further information is provided about how many units are under this bureau or how big this bureau is.[73] The bureau, through the Communications Officer Academy (통신군관학교) located in Hamhung, trains officers for its missions.[74]

ELECTRONIC WARFARE BUREAU (전자전국)

The Electronic Warfare Bureau oversees and trains all EW (electronic warfare) and electronic intelligence assets within the KPA.[75] It is reported to have been created in the mid-1980s under Kim Jong-il's orders to modernize army assets.[76] According to a 2005 briefing by the ROK Ministry of National Defense (MND), the Electronic Warfare Bureau is believed to have one EW regiment, four battalions assigned to each of the four forward-deployed corps, as wells several dozens of EW posts below the Pyongyang-Wonsan line.[77]

---

69. A South Korean news article on the General Political Bureau summarizes the lack of information and confusion about its subordinate units. The article reports the scholarship as being divided on whether the Enemy Collapse Sabotage Bureau should be placed under the General Political Bureau. See "The Second in Command within the North Korean Military Is the Director of the KPA General Political Bureau," *Tongil News*, May 3, 2014, http://www.tongilnews.com/news/quickViewArticleView.html?idxno=107136.

70. "Saenuri Party's Testifier Says 'North Korea's Cyber Agents Mess around in South Korean Online Communities,'" JTBC, August 19, 2013, http://news.jtbc.joins.com/article/article.aspx?news_id=NB10328087.

71. Bermudez, *Armed Forces of North Korea*, 34.

72. Ibid.

73. Kwan-hee Yoo, "The Truth about North Korea's 'Storm Corps,' in Charge of Creating Disturbance behind the Scenes during Wartime," *DailyNK*, March 26, 2009, http://www.dailynk.com/korean/read.php?cataId=nk04500&num=69150.

74. ROK Ministry of Unification, "North Korea Encyclopedia: Kim Il-sung Military University."

75. Bermudez, *Armed Forces of North Korea*.

76. "Mirim College: Establishment and Current Activity."

77. "North Korea's Electronic/Cyber Warfare Capabilities (Questionnaires from the Ministry of National Defense)," *News Can*, September 25, 2005, http://www.newscani.com/news/articleView.html?idxno=3375. This statement differs from Jang Se-yul's statement. A former member of one of DPRK's EW units and a North Korea defector, he said that he had heard in 2007 that KPA has two EW brigades, one in Sangwon and one in Nampo. See Ahn, "North Korea's Electronic Warfare Capability."

The objective of this unit is believed to be the disruption or destruction of the enemy's military command and control systems through electromagnetic spectrum operations such as jamming and spoofing.[78] The DPRK understands that EW is not a stand-alone tool but an element of combined arms warfare, as indicated by Kim Jong-il's statement: "Do not prepare for electronic warfare just because that is what others are doing. In modern warfare, modern and conventional weapons must be massed and combined."[79] The DPRK also seems to think about EW as both offensive and defensive measures. A leaked 2005 KPA publication titled *Electronic Warfare Reference Guide* stated, "if one disrupts the GPS [global positioning system] systems of U.S.'s precision-strike weapons, one can degrade its precision and lead it to strike another area," as well as "we can defend our troops and assets against electronically guided weapons if one knows how it works and develops appropriate defensive measures."[80]

The DPRK has used EW capabilities during real operations in the past. Although MND assessed in 2005 that it can easily defend against DPRK's EW capabilities with various countermeasures and encryption, South Korean radars were jammed in November 2010 when the DPRK fired artillery on Yeonpyeong Island.[81] During the first round of fire on November 23, South Korea's weapons-locating radar (AN/TPQ-37), which was not equipped with electronic counter-countermeasure (ECCM) capabilities, was disabled with DPRK's EW attacks. Because the radar was not able to pinpoint the location of the artillery, South Korean artillery fired to the wrong location, based on preexisting coordinates.[82] As a result, 35 out of 50 shots fired fell into the sea, and the DPRK was able to fire a second round of attacks.[83] The DPRK is believed to have conducted operational testing of its capabilities in August 2010 when several areas in the western part of South Korea reported GPS disruption.[84] In March 2011[85] and April 28 to May 14, 2012, the DPRK also sent GPS jamming signals. South Korean media reported that the military had not been affected by the signal and that many of the cruise missiles and precision-guided weapons are encrypted.[86] South Korean media reports that the DPRK uses at least two types of equipment, one imported from Russia in the early 2000s and one modified version, and that it is trying to sell the latter equipment to other countries in the Middle East.[87]

78. Bermudez, "SIGINT, EW, and EIW," 1–2.

79. Ibid.

80. Cited in Nak-gyu Yang, "Electronic Warfare Tactics as Described in North Korea's Field Manual," *Asia Economy*, April 18, 2011, http://m.asiae.co.kr/view.htm?no=2011030709432824411#cb.

81. "South Korea Loses to North Korea in Electronic Warfare . . . Radars Became Dysfunctional from North Korea's EMP Attack from North Korea's EMP Attack," *Newsis*, December 3, 2010, http://www.newsis.com/ar_detail/view.html?ar_id=NISX20101203_0006865372&cID=10211&pID=10200.

82. Suk-ho Shin and Sung-woon Yoo, "South Korea's Military Helpless Fighting Electronic Warfare," *DongA Ilbo*, December 3, 2010, http://news.donga.com/BestClick/3/all/20101203/33035628/1.

83. Ibid.

84. Ibid.

85. Yong-won Yoo, "North Korea Imports Equipment that Allows Disruption of the Entire Korean Peninsula," *Chosun Ilbo*, March 7, 2011, http://news.chosun.com/site/data/html_dir/2011/03/07/2011030700169.html.

86. Gui-geun Kim, "North Korea Halts Jamming GPS Signals after 16 Days," *Yonhap News*, May 15, 2012, http://www.yonhapnewstv.co.kr/npost/%eb%b6%81%ed%95%9c-gps-%ea%b5%90%eb%9e%80%ec%a0%84%ed%8c%8c-16%ec%9d%bc-%eb%a7%8c%ec%97%90-%ec%a4%91%eb%8b%a8/.

87. Yoo, "North Korea Imports Equipment."

Past incidents seem to indicate that the DPRK's EW capabilities can be defended against with proper encryption and ECCM. Still, the DPRK seems to be actively incorporating EW capabilities into its military operations and is continuously trying to improve its capabilities. There has been no information so far regarding whether the Electronic Warfare Bureau coordinates with other relevant cyber units for their missions, or whether it maintains some cyber capabilities in order to gain better access to its targets.

FINAL NOTES

The GSD's organizational structure indicates that the DPRK's approach to cyber warfare is more closely aligned with Chinese perspectives. China views cyber warfare as part of a holistic effort on information warfare that incorporates all aspects of affecting information such as electronic warfare, cyber warfare, and psychological operations. The U.S. perspective, however, focuses on the domain and network aspect of cyberspace to a greater extent. The operations of the Command Automation Bureau, Enemy Collapse Sabotage Bureau, Communications Bureau, and the Electronic Warfare Bureau all share a common theme in that they essentially aim to disrupt the information flow of an adversary. This also means that although these units are not strictly related to what is popularly called the cyber domain, we still need to pay attention to their combined role in being able to disrupt/destroy the use of the electromagnetic spectrum for military communications.

What is particularly interesting is not necessarily what the GSD has but what it *doesn't* have, which is a centralized cyber warfare bureau equivalent to a cyber command in other countries. Given the relatively advanced thinking on information operations and the existence of electronic warfare and psychological warfare units, it seems odd that the main military body in the country lacks a cyber warfare component. Perhaps such a unit exists within the GSD but has not yet been identified in open-source literature, or perhaps the GSD will create something similar to a cyber command in the future.

Most of the essential functions of a cyber command seem to be already carried out within the RGB instead, an organization separate from the command structure of the GSD. This can be problematic because the RGB, as a separate black ops and intelligence organization with a direct channel to senior leadership and an independent budget, is probably not beholden to the operational planning of the GSD, and a certain freedom, if one wishes to, to act independently from the larger military strategy and doctrine.

At present, the GSD is not publicly attributed with *any* disruptive cyber operations against either the United States or ROK. This could indicate that DPRK leadership conceptualizes cyber capabilities as more in line with the peacetime provocation mission of the RGB. However, one major caveat is that this is only what is reported in open-source literature. If the GSD, which is a military organization, is conducting disruptive cyber operations against sensitive military targets within the United States or ROK, these operations may not be reported. However based on open-source reporting at this time, the GSD only has active propaganda organs acting in cyberspace and any disruptive cyber capabilities, while in line with their mission and strategy, are purely theoretical.

Technology and Industrial Base

Given North Korea's prolonged isolation from the international community, discussion of North Korea's cyber capabilities has often been met with ridicule from the public. While the general level of computer technology in North Korea still lags behind the rest of the world, a close examination demonstrates that over time it has indeed developed a technology base that allows it to engage in disruptive operations sufficient for implementing its cyber strategy.[88] This technical base shows that there have been long-term attempts to build up indigenous capacity and expertise, and it is likely that this base will continue to expand and receive government attention in the future. The DPRK's software and hardware industries are worth paying attention to, as the relationship between civilian and military developers is fuzzy, especially in an authoritarian state.

Although North Korea began investing in its information technology (IT) industry as early as the 1980s, its most active efforts officially began in the late 1990s. In 1999, labeled the Year of Science, the regime established the College of Computer Science at Kim Il-sung University and the Ministry of Electric Power Industry, and declared science technology as one of the three pillars to achieve the status as a "strong and prosperous nation." Since then, it has launched a total of four five-year plans for the development of science technology, with a particular focus on computer science.[89]

Among the various government bodies, the Ministry of Posts and Telecommunications and the Ministry of Electric Power Industry oversee the development of the regime's IT industry. While the former focuses on managing and regulating various means of communication, the latter performs responsibilities more directly related to information technology, such as managing semiconductor factories and research institutions for computer science.

North Korea has systemically reinforced its IT industry centered on software development. Kim Il-sung University, Kim Chaek University, Pyongsung University of Science, Pyongyang University of Computer Technology, and all 1 Middle-high schools heavily focus on training students on software technology development. One of North Korea's achievements in software technology is computer numerical control (CNC) technology, which allowed its satellite testing. Such efforts has allowed North Korea to be at a level where it can now earn profits from sending its team of engineers to Shenyang to participate in development of programs for South Korean companies.

The DPRK regime has been pushing to improve its capabilities to manufacture hardware as well. North Korea has two factories, Pyongyang Integrated Card Factory and Tanchon Military Semiconductor Factory, which produce PCDs and basic semiconductors.

---

88. Bongsik Choi, *The North Korea Industry 2010* (Seoul: Korea Finance Corporation, 2010), http://nkinfo .unikorea.go.kr/nkp/overview/nkOverview.do?sumryMenuId=EC220.

89. ROK Ministry of Unification, "North Korea Encyclopedia: 5-Year Science Technology Development Plan," North Korea Information Portal, November 17, 2015, http://nkinfo.unikorea.go.kr/nkp/term/viewNkKnwldg Dicary.do?pageIndex=2&koreanChrctr=&dicaryId=8.

North Korea has consistently been preparing the tools and infrastructure necessary for hacking purposes. It has access to mainly two blocks of Internet protocol (IP) addresses, the first being 1,024 addresses (175.45.176.0 through 175.45.179.255) provided by Internet service provider Star Joint Venture Co. This was born out of cooperation between Korea Posts and Telecommunications Co. (KPTC) and Loxley Pacific, a firm that provides telecommunications system integration and solutions in Thailand. This block of addresses hosts many official North Korean websites, including KCNA, Naenara, the Voice of Korea, and Rodong Sinmun. Second, while lesser known, KPTC currently uses 256 China Unicom addresses (210.52.109.0 through 210.52.109.255) as well.[90]

North Korea has been developing fiber-optic cables since the 1990s centering around Pyongyang.[91] The cables facilitate the use of their intranet Kwangmyong (광명망), which is strictly monitored and controlled by the government. In addition to Kwangmyong, North Korea reportedly has three other intranets reserved for government or military purposes, namely Bangpae (방패), Geumbyeol (금별), and Bulgeungeom (붉은검).[92]

The KCC and Pyongyang Informatics Center (PIC) are the two computer centers at the core of North Korea's IT development for both hardware and software.

KOREA COMPUTER CENTER (조선콤퓨터쎈터)

The KCC was established in October 24, 1990, and is located in Sunlae-Dong, Mangyong District, Pyongyang. The KCC is a state-run IT R&D center tasked with a wide range of IT-related activities including development of computer hardware and software as well as North Korea's limited computer networks. In addition to serving an R&D function, the KCC also has authority for the production, management, distribution, and sale of its products. The KCC oversees training of IT professionals by operating centers in major universities such as Kim Chaek University and hosts a nationwide programming competition ever year.[93] The KCC oversees 9 production centers and 11 regional centers.[94] The KCC also operates at least one trading company for foreign trade, named Shinheung Trading Company.[95] A 2001 assessment estimated that the KCC had 850 personnel, about 50 with PhDs, 550 involved in software development, 100 in technology research, and 150 in development support. By 2006, the assessment had grown to about 1,200 total personnel, with around

90. Martyn Williams, "North Korea's Chinese IP Addresses," North Korea Tech, June 26, 2011, http://www.northkoreatech.org/2011/06/26/north-koreas-chinese-ip-addresses/.

91. Hyun-jeong Ryu, "Analysis of North Korea's Hacking Capabilities: Has 15-Year Cyber Combat Experience . . . Can Deal a Bigger Blow than Conventional Weapons," *ChosunBiz*, January 5, 2015, http://biz.chosun.com/site/data/html_dir/2015/01/05/2015010502512.html.

92. Soon-hyuk Lee, "Anonymous Says 'Will Launch Cyberattack against North Korea on June 25,'" *Hankyoreh*, May 8, 2013, http://www.hani.co.kr/arti/economy/it/586466.html.

93. Sung-bum Hong, "Research on the Current State of North Korea's Science Technology by Area," *Policy Research, Science and Technology Policy Institute* 1, no. 20 (January 2002): 3–4, http://www.stepi.re.kr/app/report/view.jsp?cmsCd=CM0012&categCd=A0201&ntNo=270.

94. Jong-sun Kim, "Status Quo of North Korea's Software Industry: Focusing on Analysis of the Computer OS, 'Red Star,'" *Korea Exim Bank on North Korea's Economy* (2010): 43–62, http://www.koreaexim.go.kr/kr/work/check/pub/north_view.jsp?cpage=5&bookNo=706.

95. Ibid.

100 PhDs.[96] The KCC allegedly has overseas offices and joint ventures in Germany, China, and Syria.[97] Its most well-known products include the Samjiyeon tablet PC and the Linux-based Red Star operating system (OS).

An examination of the KCC's origins and recent activities indicates that it currently seems to conduct benign IT R&D, training, production, and sales. The possibility of the KCC also serving an auxiliary/reserve role in North Korea's offensive cyber operations cannot be ruled out.

Kim Jong-nam, Kim Jong-il's first son now living in Macao and China, personally spearheaded the establishment of the KCC in the late 1980s. Kim Jong-nam was deeply involved in North Korea's national security and counterintelligence operations at the Ministry of State Security (MSS) (국가보위부) since the 1980s.[98] South Korea's National Intelligence Service (NIS) assessed in 2005 that Kim Jong-nam originally created the KCC to serve as a control tower for collecting strategic foreign intelligence and controlling domestic access to foreign information under MSS guidance.[99] After the KCC was established, Kim Jong-nam transferred the MSS's department responsible for foreign intelligence collection to the KCC.[100] Whether this collection was based solely on Internet-based open-source research or via more intrusive measures is unknown.

In the first 10 years since the KCC was established, Kim Jong-il issued over 140 personal guidances to support KCC growth as the centerpiece of North Korea's IT industry, indicating that it received the highest level of policy attention within the government.[101] In 2003, KCC's status was elevated to the "3rd Industrial General Bureau, directly under control of the Cabinet.[102]

In 2011, KCC employees operating in China were directly involved in cyber crime by developing and selling exploits that target popular games in South Korea in collaboration with Office 39, the DPRK state entity known to be responsible for earning foreign currency for the Kim family's personal account.[103] In August 2011, South Korean prosecutors indicted

96. Hong, "Research on the Current State," 29; Pil-jae Kim, *North Korea's Cyber Invasion of South Korea* (Seoul: Baeknyun Dongahn, 2014), 55; Chang-hyun Jung, "Completes Development of an Independent Computer Operating System (OS) from the Perspective of the People's Information Industry," *Minjog21*, December 13, 2012.

97. Jung, "Completes Development of Independent Computer Operating System."

98. Sung-kyu Ahn and Hyo-sik Jung, "Kim Jung-Nam Lead Establishment of KCC, the Core Effort of North Korea's Cyber Warfare," *Joongang Ilbo*, July 12, 2009, http://nk.joins.com/news/view.asp?aid=3418751.

99. So-yul Kim, "North Korea Involved in Cyber Operations in Dandong since 2004," *DailyNK*, July 12, 2009. http://www.dailynk.com/korean/read.php?cataId=nk00100&num=73841.

100. Kyo-kwan Lee, "The Secret of Korea Computer Center," *NK Chosun*, May 11, 2001, http://nk.chosun.com/news/articleView.html?idxno=6764.

101. "North Korea Elevates Its Korea Computer Center's Status to Ministerial Level," *NK Chosun*, February 21, 2001, http://nk.chosun.com/news/articleView.html?idxno=4301.

102. Taegyun Kim, "Discussion for North Korea's Development of Capacity-Building," *National Strategy* 20, no. 4 (December 2014), http://www.sejong.org/boad/bd_news/1/egofiledn.php?conf_seq=3&bd_seq=1413&file_seq=2681.

103. Suk-woo Lee, "Office 39's New Source of Revenue: Selling Hacking Programs Used in South Korean Game 'Lineage,'" *Chosun Ilbo*, August 5, 2011, http://news.chosun.com/site/data/html_dir/2011/08/05/20110 80500076.html; Kwang-young Shin and Hoon-sang Park, "The North Korean Hacker Who Targeted Online

five South Korean nationals who sold gaming exploits purchased from North Korean developers operating out of Heilongjiang Province, China. South Korean investigation revealed that around 30 North Korean hackers, operating under a cover company in China named Chosun Neungrado Trading Company, developed numerous exploits in teams of five over five months. Prosecutors announced that these developers were professional hackers selected from middle school and trained in Kim Il-sung and Kim Chaek Universities. They then were sent to work at the KCC and Neungrado Information Center under Office 39. It is important to note that the president of the trading company is listed as Park Kyu-hong, was the director of Office 39 and vice mayor of Pyongyang as of 2011.[104]

The South Korean police assessed that around 10,000 North Korean IT developers operate in China, with each required to wire $500 each month back to North Korea. About $5 million in foreign currency is generated each month if these quotas are met. The most important information from this investigation was that analysis of the exploits revealed a secondary function that allows the server port that connects the user's computer to the game's server to be open at all times, which could be used to build botnets. The Korea Internet and Security Agency (KISA) also assessed that the exploits were created by hacking the games' packet information, meaning that the North Korean hackers could see communications of the game users that could be exploited further for other attacks.[105]

This information should be taken skeptically. Although wiring back money or having wages effectively garnished by the state is consistent with numerous reports of the DPRK's monetary practices, exact numbers of workers and the exact amount sent to the DPRK are difficult to verify.

The game exploit case, however, is important for our understanding of the KCC's potential role in North Korea's cyber operations for two reasons. It indicates either that the KCC, apart from its stated mission, also supports North Korea's offensive cyber operations mission or North Korean hackers from other units frequently use KCC affiliation as a cover for their overseas operations. It would be important to find out the range and depth of the alleged collaboration between the KCC and other operational cyber units. Seeing that the KCC serves as North Korea's IT industrial base and retains a highly educated resource pool, the KCC's involvement in offensive cyber operations could mean an organizational capacity to research and develop vulnerabilities and advanced tools, conduct supply chain attacks, and serve as a way to maintain reserves in times of need.

If hackers are using KCC affiliation as a cover, South Korea's government and private-sector businesses need to consider security risks when pursuing an engagement policy aimed at furthering inter-Korean IT development projects. In the early 2000s, some South Korean software companies pursued joint projects with North Korean IT R&D centers.

Games Turned out to Be Part of an Organization Subordinate to Office 39," *DongA Ilbo*, August 5, 2011, http://news.donga.com/Politics/3/00/20110805/39319810/1.
104. Lee, "Office 39's New Source"; Shin and Park, "North Korean Hacker."
105. Shin and Park, "North Korean Hacker."

Korea Computer Center's KCC 1 Production Guidance Bureau Organization

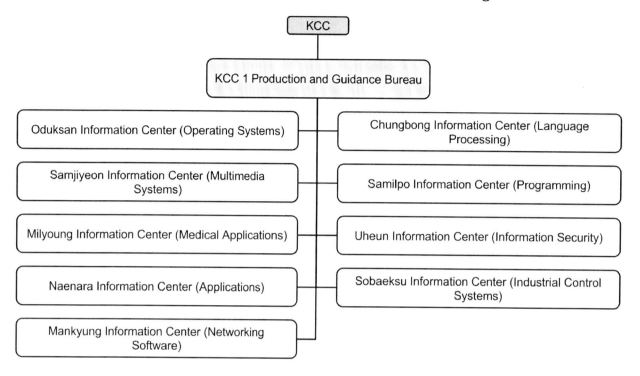

Source: Chang-nyong Suh, "North Korea via the Internet," iNews24, October 15, 2003, http://opinion.inews24.com/php /view_print.php?g_serial=100874&g_menu=041700&pay_news=0&access; "Korea Computer Center," http://www .dprksearch.net/bbs/skin/ggambo7002_board/print.php?id=dprklive&no=40.

Academics visited Pyongyang to provide training and education for North Korean IT professionals. Unwanted technology transfers may have occurred as well. This is not to say that all collaboration is harmful, but a process should be in place that weighs the potential benefits of such collaboration with its risks.

The game exploit case illustrates that the organizational distinction between cyber crime, espionage, and offensive operations are not clear-cut in North Korea. In the United States, officials often get hung up on categorizing a particular action in cyberspace as crime, espionage, or war (which is further divided into discussions on its degree of severity according to international law), because such categorization is helpful for assigning responsibilities to a particular bureaucracy. There is a proclivity to delineate in an effort to render cybersecurity more manageable, which leaves the U.S. bureaucracy in a weak position to understand hybrid cyber threats unless information is shared in an adequate and timely manner.

An authoritarian regime, such as North Korea with its very small decision-making circle, can pursue a strictly objective-oriented strategy and redirect various resources toward that objective as needed, rather than being organizationally confined. North Korean decisionmakers do not need to have intense discussions about whether a particular action in cyberspace is Title 10 or Title 50 authority. Activities such as cyber crime and hacktivism are not confined to non-state actors, nor are functions of espionage and military action strictly delineated. Especially after the centralization of cyber and clandestine capabilities under the RGB, criminal activities (e.g., selling malicious gaming software) can have the dual functions of espionage or botnet building for further exploitation, because it is entirely possible for information gathered from espionage to be fed back to organizations for criminal purposes or offensive operations. At the same time, one cyber unit can be engaged in all three arenas—generating the department's revenue via cyber crime, exfiltrating data, and conducting offensive operations—depending on what the mission requires. This organizational culture is fundamentally different from how U.S. operates in cyberspace, and needs to be taken into account when formulating a cyber strategy vis-à-vis North Korea.

PYONGYANG INFORMATICS CENTER (평양정보센터)

The PIC was established in July 1986 and is located in Kyungheung-Dong, Botonggang District, Pyongyang. It was modeled after the Osaka Information Center (OIC) within Osaka University of Economics and Law.[106] The PIC's mission is narrower than that of the KCC, focusing primarily on software programming. The PIC is led by Choi Joo-sik, its inaugural director, and has grown from a small lab of 7 employees to about 520 personnel, including 180 researchers of which 30 have PhDs. Most are around 20 to 30 years old.[107] The PIC is credited with developing several software programs widely used in North Korea, including the Changduk word processing software and Dangun program for Korean language processing. The PIC maintains offices in Singapore and Japan.[108] At this point, there is no evidence to indicate that the PIC is explicitly engaged in malicious cyber activity.

The PIC served as one of the primary centers of inter-Korean IT cooperation in the early 2000s as a part of South Korea's Sunshine Policy.[109] While small-scale exchanges occurred before, cooperation was encouraged as part of a larger economic engagement policy with North Korea after the inter-Korean summit in June 2000, focusing on joint software R&D and training. Support for these efforts gradually waned after North Korea's first nuclear test in 2006 and Lee Myung-bak's election as South Korea's president in 2008. Support ceased after North Korea's torpedo attack against the *Cheonan* in March 2010. Subsequently, the South Korean government issued the 5.24 sanctions, banning all inter-Korean trade, investment, unapproved humanitarian aid, and visits.

106. "Pyongyang Informatics Center," *Digital North Korea Encyclopedia*, https://web.archive.org/web/20150505204551/http://www.kplibrary.com/nkterm/read.aspx?num=989.

107. "What Is Pyongyang Informatics Center Like?," *ET News*, February 12, 2001, http://www.etnews.com/200102110005?SNS=00002.

108. Ibid.

109. This not to say that the PIC was the only organization to cooperate with South Korean organizations. The KCC collaborated with both Samsung Electronics and Korea Telecom (KT), and there was an educational exchange between South Korea's Hanyang University and Kim Chaek University. See Chan-mo Park, "New Prospects in Science Technology Cooperation between North and South Korea" (presentation at Forum on Science Technology Policy hosted by Science and Technology Policy Institute, Seoul, South Korea, 2012), http://www.stepi.re.kr/module/forumDownFile.jsp?cmsCd=CM0037&ntNo=14999&sbNo=1&fileFlag=spk.

One of the most significant examples is the North-South joint operation of the Hana Program Center in Dandong, Liaoning Province, China, from 2001 to 2011. The center was established through a 4:6 joint investment totaling $2 million by the PIC and Hanabiz, a South Korean holding company for a consortium of 30 private companies, one public organization, and two nongovernmental organizations (NGOs).[110] The basic business model was to combine South Korea's capital with North Korean labor to produce competitive software products. Hanabiz was to win software development contracts from South Korean companies, jointly develop products with PIC employees, and train PIC employees at the Hana Program Center. The original vision was that Dandong could grow as a IT R&D hub modeled after California's Silicon Valley, and eventually contribute to the development of the nearby Sinuiju Special Administrative Region (SAR) in North Korea.[111] South Korea's Ministry of Unification, under its budget allocated for North-South cooperation, provided annual funding to Hanabiz for training North Korean IT professionals from 2005 to2009, a total of slightly less than $0.5 million.[112]

Although the company eventually failed to attract contracts and ceased operations in 2011, examining the Hana Program Center's operations provides a rare opportunity to evaluate how sophisticated North Korea's most elite IT professionals are. Below is a selection of evaluations from several records of site visits and interviews with members of the Hana Program Center.

- In 2008, a team from Korea Development Institute (KDI) made a site visit to the Hana Program Center. They reported that around 200 personnel had been trained at the center thus far and 70 North Korean employees currently worked there. The software programming capabilities were "fairly high." Employees were paid more than $200 a month, much higher than the average wage of around $60 for workers at the Kaesong industrial complex.[113]

- In a 2004 interview, Moon Gwang-seung, director of the Hana Program Center, said that the skills of North Korea's software engineers "aren't much different" from their South Korean counterparts, except when it comes to user interface designs because that requires thinking from the consumer's perspective. Thus, most of the joint development had been focused on improving Linux capabilities and software for network devices rather than application software. Interestingly, he also stated that North Korea seems to be more advanced than South Korea in terms of information security technology.[114]

110. Hyun-jin Seo, "Terms of Agreements Regarding 'Hana Program Center,' the First IT Joint-Venture between North and South Korea," *Minjog21*, May 1, 2001, http://www.minjog21.com/news/quickViewArticleView .html?idxno=597.

111. Ibid.

112. Seong-wook Kim, "Roh Administration Found to Have Funded Training of North Korea's IT Human Resources Annually," *New Daily*, June 1, 2010, http://www.newdaily.co.kr/news/article.html?no=37882.

113. Seok Lee and Sang-ki Kim, "Report on Travels from China (Shenyang and Dandong)" (Seoul: Korea Development Institute, 2008), https://www.kdi.re.kr/data/download/attach/12241_28.pdf, 7.

114. Seunghyun Lee, "Despite Many Talks, HanaBiz the Only Outcome from Economic Cooperation between North and South Korea," *Tongil News*, March 24, 2004, http://www.tongilnews.com/news/articleView .html?idxno=42717.

- In another 2004 interview with Radio Free Asia, Moon said that there were 23 full-time North Korean employees at the center, and all possessed master's or PhD degrees and more than five years of work experience.[115]

- In 2001, a South Korean newspaper reported accounts of several South Korean IT experts who taught the first class of 30 North Koreans at the center. The students were from the PIC, Kim Il-sung University, Kim Chaek University, University of Natural Science, and University of Computer Technology. Although not considered the most elite, they possessed advanced skills. The general evaluation was that they are "persistent and had a good grasp of the basics." One expert said they would be competitive after four to six months of training, and another expert was surprised at their tenaciousness in completing assignments.[116]

The Hana Program Center was operated in tandem with educational exchanges between the PIC and South Korea's Pohang University of Science and Technology (POSTECH) via Park Chan-mo, POSTECH's president. In April 2001, Choi (the PIC's director) and Park signed an agreement for joint R&D and related training in Pyongyang and Dandong, with POSTECH providing the financing.[117] One of the most significant outcomes from this engagement was the establishment of the state-of-the-art Pyongyang University of Science and Technology (PUST) in 2010, where Park serves as chancellor. PUST has four departments: information communication technology, agricultural & food technology, industrial management, and basic education. All coursework is allegedly taught in English, mostly by foreign professors.[118] As of 2013, PUST had 300 undergraduate students and 78 graduate students. All were selected through the recommendation of the North Korean Ministry of Education.[119]

FINAL NOTES

North Korea, despite what may be expected, has a technical base for both hardware and software development. While it is not as robust or well developed as those in China, South Korea, or the United States, North Korea's technology sector has domestic support and does not follow the stereotype of being technologically and intellectually starved. Thinking that the DPRK is incapable of technological and computer development would be incorrect and lead to inaccurate conclusions.

---

115. Soo-kyung Lee, "HanaBiz Establishes Hana Program Center, a Joint-Venture between North and South Korea in China, and Initiates Training on Information and Communication," Radio Free Asia, 2004, http://www.rfa.org/korean/in_focus/89456-20020913.html.

116. Jae-kwon Jung, "We have Witnessed the Potential of North Korea's IT Human Resources," *Hankyoreh*, October 29, 2001, http://legacy.www.hani.co.kr/section-003100000/2001/10/003100000200110290350027.html.

117. Park, "New Prospects in Science Technology Cooperation," 35.

118. Geun-tae Park, "Information on Pyongyang University of Science Technology, Where Google's CEO Has Recently Made a Visit," *ChosunBiz*, January 9, 2013, http://biz.chosun.com/site/data/html_dir/2013/01/09/2013010902018.html.

119. Ibid.

3 | Future Trends and Policy Recommendations

This report has thus far established that cyber operations are a critical component of North Korea's overarching national strategy. This trajectory will continue unless there is a significant change in the status quo. This indicates that interested parties must reflect on the strategic implications of the regime's pursuit of cyber warfare capabilities. North Korea is often referred to in policy circles as a "land of lousy options," and dealing with cyber attacks from North Korea is not an exception. Finding a legal and public response to a cyber attack that falls below the use of force threshold is difficult. However, there are options available to policymakers that should be examined. This chapter will outline some options policymakers and officials have in dealing with North Korea's cyber capabilities. Four basic policy objectives aimed at managing the emerging cyber threat from North Korea are discussed. Subsequently, ways these objectives can be met are explored, from a U.S. perspective and a U.S.-ROK alliance perspective.

There is little reason to believe that the DPRK will cease to invest in cyber operations capabilities in the future. It has had a long history of relying on violence for coercion and there is little indication that this will change. Offensive cyber operations offer a new means of achieving old goals at lower cost and operational risk. North Korea may also believe that cyber operations could provide a means of extended power projection and coercion, especially against states otherwise difficult to reach such as the United States. So far, responses from U.S. or South Korean governments after suffering cyber attacks from North Korea did not seem to convince North Korea that relying on cyber means for provocations was a bad idea, and may have actually convinced North Korea that cyber means are excellent asymmetric tools. Unlike after the 2010 Yeonpyong Island incident when the U.S.-ROK alliance relatively quickly decided on enhanced rules of engagement, the intricacies of the cyber domain and the lack of widely accepted international norms on appropriate responses to a low intensity cyber attack means that policy and strategic responses to North Korea's cyber operations will require more creativity and insights from multiple disciplines.

Future Trends

If left unrestrained, North Korea is likely to continue to place strategic value in its cyber capabilities and will continue to conduct cyber operations in the future. Future potential operations could be a continuation of low-intensity operations or an escalation to higher-intensity attacks that approach or cross the use of force threshold. While the lower-intensity options are more probable because continued small provocations are less likely to risk an escalatory response from the U.S. and ROK, planners should prepare for scenarios of spikes in intensity based on a history of unexpected provocations by North Korea. Furthermore, alongside the continuation of disruptive cyber operations, the DPRK could deepen the integration of cyber capabilities with its conventional military force for their use in military operations.

A SPECTRUM OF INTENSITY

Future DPRK cyber operations could occur along a spectrum of intensity. At one end is a continuation of relatively low-intensity operations that rarely or never clearly rise to the use of force threshold. On the other end is an increase in the intensity of operations from the current pattern of attacks to an operation that may cross the use of force threshold.

Keeping operations at a low intensity allows DPRK's cyber operations to continue at a level that may be begrudgingly accepted by the United States and ROK due to the lack of readily available legal and public responses and the potential ineffectiveness of sanctions regimes in inducing these operations to stop. This keeps the United States and ROK, unless their policies change, in the position of being repeatedly assailed by such attacks without concrete mechanisms to effectively respond. This situation would allow the DPRK to continuously harass the United States and ROK, potentially costing both governments as well as private companies millions of dollars. This also could elicit clandestine responses from the United States and ROK, but these would likely be occurring outside international norms and legal frameworks.

One important side effect may be a psychological erosion of faith in cyberspace as a reliable and safe medium for conducting daily business. Even though high-profile disruptive cyber operations may remain at a low intensity, problems may arise if attacks occur repeatedly. Although each incident individually will be recoverable, the repetition of such operations can lead to an increasingly unreliable business or operating environment. Here, high-profile means that the operations are well publicized and covered in the media. The actual effects may have been isolated or minimally damaging to the economy, as was the case in the 2014 Sony Pictures Entertainment attack. The problem becomes one less about grave economic damages or physical damage of property and more about the need to maintain the public's confidence and trust.

At the other end of the spectrum is an increase in the intensity of operations from the current pattern of attacks to an operation that may cross the use of force threshold. This is a worst-case scenario in which North Korea, emboldened from past successful cyber operations or miscalculation, decides to pursue more damaging cyber operations against the United States or ROK. The lack of precedents and international agreements on responding to various scenarios of such a cyber operation may risk leading to an escalated scenario outside the control of any parties involved.

Miscalculations and miscommunication can lead to an extreme case. A lack of clear normative or legal boundaries can lead to underestimating the severity of an operation's consequences, or could lead to a total misreading of the level of tension on the Korean peninsula. For certain types of cyber attacks, the potential for unintended collateral damage also cannot be ruled out, where the damage incurred may be much greater than what North Korea initially intended. A lack of preexisting declared policies regarding how a state will respond to cyber operations of varying intensity could fail to adequately inform the North Korea regarding the direct repercussions associated with such an attack.

A move towards more destructive cyber operations would likely also restrict North Korea's freedom to execute low-intensity operations as well, because the U.S. and ROK may be incentivized to respond by restricting North Korea's ability to operate in general. However, such operations are still not unthinkable, especially as an accident or one-off provocation. Although the 2010 shelling of Yeonpyeong Island was not expected, it was not a strategic surprise because the United States and ROK prepare for worst-case scenarios to arise occasionally. Additionally, an escalated and intense cyber operation would not be a strategic surprise, though it would certainly be an operational surprise. Tensions are common on the Korean peninsula and between the DPRK and United States, sometimes leading to crises or additional provocations. In the future, these could include cyber operations or cyber operations alongside more conventional military operations.

Spikes of high-intensity operations should be prepared for, regardless of their cause. In a similar manner to how U.S. and ROK armed forces prepare for worst-case scenarios involving conventional forces, they and the civilian government should prepare for a variety of high-intensity cyber operations or conventional provocations that include cyber elements. Priority should be placed upon critical infrastructure targets, especially those that are essential during armed conflict for logistical and communications. When appropriate, declaratory policy regarding the appropriate responses should be released to clarify government responses and attempt to establish some sort of clear chain of responses.

As long as North Korea continues to develop its cyber capabilities in accordance with its national strategy, all points on the cyber attack intensity spectrum must be considered. Realistically, the future will see low-intensity incidents, possibly with brief, probing high intensity attacks, or a slow increase in intensity. The DPRK's doctrine and technology will also become more sophisticated. Perhaps normative behavior will eventually arise from low-intensity exchanges and operations, but the United States and especially the ROK must be prepared for continued North Korean operations and worst-case scenarios.

INTEGRATION WITH NON-CYBER OPERATIONS

Concurrently, the DPRK may move away from pure cyber operations and increase integration of cyber capabilities into military operations. Even before North Korea developed cyber capabilities it has had a well-established tradition of planning to utilize irregular operations in armed conflict. However, achieving such integration requires significant sophistication in military strategy and doctrine and would also require joint training and exercises before capabilities are seamlessly integrated. Policymakers should expect a potential combination of cyber operations with information operations and electronic warfare (EW), as well as complements to missions to degrade and disrupt air and missile defense systems or logistics and communications networks.

If the United States and ROK do work out ways of containing and mitigating asymmetric cyber operations, the Korean People's Army (KPA) may become a more conventional cyber power with cyber units integrated in a similar fashion to embedded electronic and political warfare units. The DPRK's treatment of EW could be a thematic template for future military cyber operations. As mentioned in Chapter 1, the DPRK emphasizes asymmetric capabilities in its military as a means of fighting more effectively against a superior opponent. However, there is no indication in the open-source literature that this evolution has already occurred within the DPRK military.

Future signposts for operational integration could be events such as network and radar issues occurring concurrently with missile tests. Signposts for military integration could be cyclical or repeated issues with air and missile defense networks, including radar systems and other military sensors. What North Korea may be targeting may also lend insight to their evolving strategy, such as signs of attempted compromise in military command and control centers and networks or tactical data links. Especially notable would be issues that arise on major political anniversaries of North Korean or inter-Korea events. Additionally, the appearance of cyber exercises in North Korean military exercises could be indicative of operational integration of cyber units into conventional military formations, though this would not be information available in open-source literature.

Policy Objectives

There are four main policy objectives for managing the emerging North Korean threat in cyberspace, none of which should be pursued exclusively. Specific policy recommendations for the United States and the U.S.-ROK alliance are then discussed with these four general objectives in mind.

1. **Prepare a graduated series of direct responses targeting North Korea's cyber organizations.** As previously noted, there is always a chance that DPRK cyber operations will escalate in intensity, either due to emboldenment or miscalculation. The United States and U.S.-ROK alliance must prepare a variety of response options appropriate to the intensity of a situation. For both defense planning and deterrence purposes, it is important to prepare responses for a wide range of operations, from low intensity to high intensity. For defense planning, it is important to have exercise and training for various crises scenarios, whether these involve very damaging attacks or low-level harassment. For deterrence, establishing and clearly communicating a response policy helps to mitigate misinformation or misinformed guessing about U.S. and ROK responses to certain operations, potentially changing the cost and risk perceptions for DPRK cyber units.

2. **Curb North Korea's operational freedom in cyberspace.** North Korea currently faces little barriers to conducting cyber operations. It has allegedly been able to physically locate units outside of its own national territory and continues to enjoy the institutional and economic support of the organization it is housed under, the Reconnaissance General Bureau. In addition to trying to deter a cyber attack and to impose costs in response to an attack, proactive law enforcement efforts to curb North Korea's resources associated with cyber operations may have an impact of its own.

3. **Identify and leverage North Korea's vulnerabilities to maintain strategic balance.** A cyber operation would not have the same effect on the DPRK as it does against the ROK. While the United States and ROK are heavily dependent on networks and high-tech infrastructure both for civilian and military affairs, the DPRK is not. Responding to cyber operations against the United States or ROK with cyber operations against North Korea would not have the same proportionate effect. Therefore, responses should be tailored to leverage North Korea's specific weaknesses and sensitivities. North Korea has unique asymmetric vulnerabilities as well, especially to outside information that attacks the legitimacy of the regime.

4. **Adopt damage mitigation and resiliency measures to ensure that critical systems and networks maintain operational continuity during and after an attack.** The United States and ROK are not at the point technologically or strategically to prevent operations from being conducted or from causing damage. As such, entities should expect that some operations will get through and do damage.

Recommendations for the United States

The United States and ROK have several options available to help curb North Korea's cyber operations, including sanctions, targeting the DPRK's asymmetric information vulnerability, and pushing for stronger adoption and enactment of international laws and norms regarding state obligations in cyberspace. These solutions will not be perfect and will not stand alone. A creative combination of responses is needed. Policymakers with access to accurate intelligence estimates need to determine what the optimal application of pressure is.

ESTABLISH DECLARATORY POLICIES

The United States should consider developing a declared policy on the U.S. range of countermeasures for low-intensity cyber attacks qualifying as internationally wrongful acts. After the cyber attack against Sony in November 2014, U.S. policymakers did not have an established menu of proportional response options, thus hindering the ability of the United States to respond quickly and send a clear signal. Establishing a declared policy allows for more timely responses and may have deterrent effects. These positives outweigh the negatives of potentially binding one's hands, so long as the government is willing and able to execute its own policy. Measures such as Executive Order (EO) 13694, announced on

April 1, 2015, have prepared the groundwork for such a policy, but further explicit responses should be set so that U.S. entities are prepared to respond quickly in future crises. As these response measures would address low-intensity cyber attacks, policy should distinguish countermeasures (e.g., sanctions) from peacetime reprisals (e.g., armed attacks).

Two forms of responses are reprisals and countermeasures, both of which are retaliatory responses. Reprisals are illegal armed retaliations in peacetime, while countermeasures are non-armed responses, such as sanctions, that can be switched off once the offending state comes back into compliance with international law.

The idea behind countermeasures is that a nation should not engage in tit-for-tat armed attacks, but instead should put some sort of nonviolent pressure upon the offending country until it comes back into compliance with international law. The concept is that instead of retaliatory attacks, states are supposed to focus on compliance with norms and law, which theoretically would help resolve a dispute without a high risk of escalation. This is a particularly desirable situation on the Korean peninsula, which is known to be tense and prone to escalation over petty political disputes.

These ideas are represented in the Draft Articles of State Responsibility, and U.S. policymakers have considered the document's application in cyberspace. The Draft Articles of State Responsibility note that in general, it is illegal for a state to launch an unlawful action (reprisals) against another state in peacetime. Currently, the vast majority of disruptive or destructive cyber attacks have not reached a use of force or armed-attack threshold. The concept of countermeasures, if framed and used properly in tandem with state due diligence regarding cyber attacks, may provide states a reasonable mechanism for responding to an internationally wrongful cyber operation during peacetime.

While countermeasures can be a useful policy option in bringing an offending state back into compliance with international laws and norms, numerous safeguards against their abuse limits its role as a broad policy tool for retaliating to any type of low-intensity cyber operation. Countermeasures are supposed to be appropriately *proportional* to the injury suffered so victimized states cannot leverage ridiculous or disproportionate sanctions for minor attacks. The instances where one can resort to countermeasures is highly restrictive so as to prevent state abuse and exploitation of otherwise legitimate countermeasures. The Draft Articles of State Responsibility delineates that countermeasuresmust be:[1]

- Refraining from threat or use of force (Article 50)[2]

- Proportional to the injury suffered, quantitatively and qualitatively (Article 51)[3]

---

1. United Nations, *UN Legislative Series: Materials on the Responsibility of States for Internationally Wrongful Acts* (New York, 2012), http://legal.un.org/legislativeseries/documents/Book25/Book25.pdf.
2. Ibid., 316.
3. Ibid., 324.

- Directed only against the responsible state, though may incidentally affect the position of third parties (Article 49)[4]

- Intended to be instrumental in bringing cessation and reparation rather than punishment, thus temporary and reversible as much as possible (Article 49)

- Not in violation of certain basic obligations, such as human rights (Article 50)[5]

- The intent to take countermeasures should be notified and given a chance to negotiate (Article 52)[6]

- Ceased "without undue delay" if the internationally wrong act has ceased or is pending before a court (Article 52)[7]

Countermeasures can be:[8]

1. An otherwise unlawful action, thus contrasted with merely unfriendly conduct (retorsion)

2. Not necessarily restricted to "reciprocal countermeasures," or the suspension of the same obligation that has been breached

Though these concepts are fairly simple, it is difficult to determine where cyber operations fit in regards to uses of force and what the least amount of damage done is required for an incident in cyberspace to count as a use of force or armed-attack. Policymakers should keep these notions in mind, even if an exact answer is difficult to come by.

The above requirements for being able to resort to countermeasures means that countermeasures cannot be used as a broad policy tool in response to all instances or types of cyber attacks that fall below the use of force threshold. Countermeasures could not be used in the case of incidents that do not constitute violation of sovereignty nor an international wrongful act under the conditions described above. There is considerable danger in regarding countermeasures as a blank check for retaliation, though countermeasures offer a more legitimate and less risky means of conflict resolution than unilateral action.

Based on these considerations, relevant agencies in the U.S. government should be engaged in a discussion on whether and what parts of the Draft Articles of State Responsibility may be useful in setting new norms and standards regarding disruptive cyber activities. Results of the Tallinn 2.0 discussions may be particularly relevant in advancing this discussion. The benefits of accepting clearer international rules regarding low-intensity cyber attacks should be weighed against the costs of binding one's own hands. The results of these internal deliberations should be made public as a declaratory policy, and endorsed in future relevant global and regional forums.

---

4. Ibid., 310.
5. Ibid., 316.
6. Ibid., 329.
7. Ibid.
8. Ibid.

The benefits of establishing such a policy is that it can send a stronger signal to the adversary that even low-intensity cyber attacks falling below the use of force threshold may have negative consequences, possibly altering the cost/benefit calculus of the adversary in deciding to carry out such an attack. The signal would probably not be so strong as to create a strong deterrent effect for low-intensity cyber attacks, but it would add a degree of complexity in the adversary's decisionmaking process.

IMPLEMENT SANCTIONS

The United States should further implement EO 13687 and 13694 against specific DPRK individuals and/or entities that have engaged in cyber attacks that pose a threat to national security. Sanctions are the most well-known and frequently employed countermeasure. Ideally, sanctions economically burden targeted individuals and organizations until compliance is reached, at which time the sanctions are repealed. The clandestine and military nature of North Korea's cyber capabilities make them particularly difficult to punish with sanctions.

Executive Orders 13687 and 13694 provide the U.S. Treasury with the explicit authority to pursue sanctions against the Reconnaissance General Bureau and individuals and entities involved in disruptive cyber operations. EO 13687 specifically targets the RGB and related leadership, while EO 13694 targets individuals that can be proven to be involved in disruptive cyber operations. Together, these EOs enable the U.S. executive to increase the operating costs of North Korea's disruptive cyber operations.[9]

However, the United States faces great difficulty in implementing these sanctions. Specifically identifying individuals within the RGB for targeted sanctions is difficult and the issue of individual targeting is a large obstacle to successful action. EOs 13687 and 13694 need more information to successfully apply them in any relevant way. The RGB may maintain shell and front companies not openly known, including older companies renamed in order to dodge sanctions research. More public release of intelligence information, as well as general information, is needed to pinpoint who is involved in these operations and who can legally be targeted.

Indicting and issuing warrants for the arrest of known perpetrators of illicit cyber activities is another option that the U.S. could follow if it can successfully investigate, gather enough targeting information, and share such evidences with the public. As happened with the U.S. indictment of the five Chinese People's Liberation Army (PLA) military hackers in 2014, little practical effect would be achieved at first. However, it would continue building precedent for rule of law over cyber activities and create additional friction

---

9. U.S. President, Executive Order, "Blocking the Property of Certain Persons Engaging in Significant Malicious Cyber-Enabled Activities," *Federal Register* 80, no. 18077 (April 2, 2015): 13694, https://www .federalregister.gov/articles/2015/04/02/2015-07788/blocking-the-property-of-certain-persons-engaging-in -significant-malicious-cyber-enabled-activities; U.S. President, Executive Order, "Imposing Additional Sanctions with Respect to North Korea," *Federal Register* 80, no. 817 (January 6, 2015): 13687, https://www .federalregister.gov/articles/2015/01/06/2015-00058/imposing-additional-sanctions-with-respect-to-north -korea.

for any targeted officials attempting to travel abroad in contravention of sanctions because they could possibly be targeted for criminal prosecution or attempted extradition.

The U.S. Department of Justice should have grounds to issue warrants when attribution to specific hackers can be confirmed. One of the charges for the PLA hackers was the transmission of "conspiring to commit computer fraud and abuse" under 18 U.S. Code (U.S.C.) § 1030(b),[10] something that literally describes part of the process for a cyber operation that exploits a foreign business's networks. There are numerous other statutes that could be applicable, especially if operations continue or escalate within U.S. territory.

In terms of traditional sanctions, North Korea at large, the RGB, RGB leadership, and numerous other government and party officials are already targeted for sanctions by the United Nations, United States, and other nations. However, these sanctions are very broad in scope and description and none are explicitly tied to the reduction or elimination of malicious cyber operations, which again brings up the issue of individual targeting. A clear link to the specific units blamed for cyber attacks needs be established, with supporting attributive proof, to strengthen the enforcement of sanctions and gain international support.

Even if the specific identification of sanctionable individuals is possible, the application and effectiveness of sanctions is not without problems. Verification of sanctions is difficult, if not impossible. Possibly some sort of probationary period may be required in which activities are heavily monitored and in the event of another attributable offensive operation, sanctions would continue. Sanctions are notoriously difficult to enforce and rarely change behavior in the desired manner.[11]

North Korea is already heavily sanctioned. Despite—or perhaps partially because of— these heavy sanctions, it continues provocative and internationally illegal activities. Sanctions mixed with additional pressures may have a better chance of succeeding whereas sanctions alone will fail. It is difficult to achieve behavioral change without added military pressure, internal opposition to government, and comprehensive international isolation.[12]

North Korea's harsh treatment of internal dissent puts it on a fine line between "no viable opposition" and "borderline revolting opposition" that is very difficult to define. Sanctions mixed with some sort of information campaign might result in enough pressure for behavior change. The recent purge of numerous government, party, and military officials and the rapidly changing roster of leadership means that the government structure may be particularly vulnerable to the types internal shocks that could be generated by sanctions and additional pressures.

---

10. U.S. Department of Justice, *U.S. Charges Five Chinese Military Hackers for Cyber Espionage against U.S. Corporations and a Labor Organization for Commercial Advantage*," May 19, 2014, http://www.justice.gov/opa/pr /us-charges-five-chinese-military-hackers-cyber-espionage-against-us-corporations-and-labor.

11. Peter Wallensteen, *A Century of Economic Sanctions: A Field Revisited* (Uppsala: Uppsala University, 2000), 5.

12. Ibid., 10–17.

Much like sanctions and political pressure against Yugoslavia in the 1990s, pressure from a friendly big power, be it China or Russia, could be a vital boon in achieving compliance. However this is a highly political problem that can be hamstrung by other complicated geopolitical problems.

Additionally, sanctions should be sticky and smart, meaning that they are specifically targeted to the relevant entities and revised as entities or economies adapt to deal with the sanctions. Sanctions that are enforced statically for too long can eventually be adapted to and sidestepped by an active economy, rendering the sanctions irrelevant or less effective.

Sanctions overall are difficult to enforce for an already sanctioned and besieged country such as North Korea. A mix of external and internal pressures along with sanctions that are explicitly tied to goals of compliance may be more effective than current broad and goal-less sanctions being applied to North Korea.

STRENGTHEN NORMS OF STATE BEHAVIOR IN CYBERSPACE

The United States should promote strengthening the international legal and normative base in order to curb North Korea's current operational freedom with a wider range of policy options. International adoption of state responsibility in cyberspace places a due diligence obligation on states to ensure, within their respective capacity, that cyber infrastructure within their jurisdiction is not knowingly used for malicious purposes. This can form a legal and normative basis for assigning culpability to North Korea for failing to hold up its obligations to not launch malicious cyber activities from its territory. It also forms a basis for curbing North Korea's potential overseas cyber operational bases by imposing the same obligation on third-party states to ensure that cyber infrastructure within their territory is not being used for malicious cyber activity against other states.

Part of the difficulty in finding ways to respond appropriately to the November 2014 cyber attack against Sony was in the considerable uncertainty surrounding international laws and norms regarding what states legally can or cannot do in response to a cyber attack that causes damage, but not so grave as amounting to the use of force or an armed attack. For the lack of a better term, President Obama called the incident cyber vandalism,[13] a phrase that is more significant for what it does not mean than what it does mean. One of the more interesting ways the Sony incident has been characterized was that it was a violation of sovereignty as a result of an internationally wrongful act, if it is accepted that the attack is attributable to a state and accept that a sufficient breach of sovereignty occurs when physical damage has resulted.[14] In such a case, international legal experts have argued that the customary law Draft Articles on State Responsibility[15] may be

---

13. Eric Bradner, "Obama: North Korea's Hack Not War, but 'Cybervandalism'," CNN, December 24, 2014, http://www.cnn.com/2014/12/21/politics/obama-north-koreas-hack-not-war-but-cyber-vandalism.

14. Michael Schmitt, "International Law and Cyber Attacks: Sony v. North Korea," Just Security, December 17, 2014, https://www.justsecurity.org/18460/international-humanitarian-law-cyber-attacks-sony-v-north-korea.

15. United Nations, "Materials on the Responsibility of States."

a suitable existing international legal framework to apply. Preliminary discussions for Tallinn 2.0 are taking a closer look at this.[16]

The Draft Articles on State Responsibility allow culpability and response options to be delineated for malicious cyber activities classified as violations of sovereignty and internationally wrongful acts. Adoption and entrenchment of the concepts of the Draft Articles on State Responsibility would mean that the next time a Sony-style attack occurs, the United States can, once the perpetrator is attributed properly, quickly move toward a formal legal redress.

One of the core concepts behind applying Draft Articles on State Responsibility to cyber attacks is the notion that a state has both rights as well as duties in exercising its sovereignty. If applied to cyberspace, this would mean that each state has a due diligence to take appropriate measures within its capacity to ensure that its territory is not knowingly used to conduct cyber attacks against other states.[17] The failure of a state to meet this obligation would provide the victim state a legal basis to seek remedies, either in the form of reparations (Articles 34–39)[18] or countermeasures against the responsible state in order to ensure cessation of malicious activity and compliance of its reparations duties (Articles 49–54).[19] The application of this concept is limited to cases in which the responsible state has committed an internationally wrongful act, which means that elements of the attack has to be attributable to a state (Articles 4–11) and constitutes a breach of an international obligation.

As with all international obligations, applying state due diligence in cyberspace comes with both advantages and disadvantages. However, for a country that heavily relies on cyberspace for military, political, economic, and cultural activity and faces asymmetric threats exploiting this dependence, there are perhaps more gains to be made from delineating rights and duties in this regard rather than leaving it to ad hoc policy responses without mechanisms for crisis management. The establishment of rights and duties should not be simply thought of as binding states, but as establishing a mechanism for states to seek reasonable remedies for injuries from relatively low-intensity cyber attacks without risking escalation and setting prior expectations about the consequences of launching cyber attacks. Risk-aversive, status quo–oriented states especially have more to gain from this framework, by having more options to respond rather than just offensive actions.

Establishment of state due diligence in cyberspace may help curb North Korea's cyber operations in the long term in a number of ways. First, it would form a basis for limiting North Korea's overseas bases of cyber operations. Under this framework, states would have an obligation to not knowingly allow malicious cyber operations to emanate from their

16. Ashley Deeks, "Tallinn 2.0 and a Chinese View on the Tallinn Process," *Lawfare*, May 31, 2015, http://www.lawfareblog.com/tallinn-20-and-chinese-view-tallinn-process.

17. Michael N. Schmitt, "In Defense of Due Diligence in Cyberspace," *Yale Law Journal*, June 22, 2015, http://www.yalelawjournal.org/forum/in-defense-of-due-diligence-in-cyberspace.

18. United Nations "Materials on the Responsibility of States," 220–259.

19. Ibid., 304–339.

territory, and the victim state would have a right to notify such state of the fact and request compliance. This provides the victim state a basis for complaint, and a right to use countermeasures when a breach of the obligation continues. After notification, the burden would rest on the harboring state, not the victim state, to ensure within its capacity that the malicious activity ceases, irrespective of whether the actor is a non-state, state, or third-party actor. The adoption of such a framework can also help form a stronger basis for declaratory policies regarding responding to a low-intensity cyber attack.

A possible corollary to state due diligence is that it may help further clarify the rights and duties of neutral or transit states, which would further incentivize states to not knowingly harbor foreign cyber units within their territory. In the long term, this framework can foster greater international cooperation after a cyber attack, especially on incident response.

PROMOTE INTERNATIONAL COOPERATION

The United States should promote policies for international cooperation. Unless the objective of the measures are purely to send a message to the DPRK in order to produce a deterrent effect for specific types of disruptive cyber operations, unilateral action will have limited real impact on curbing North Korea's cyber operations. Imperative for a unified front, international cooperation is also necessary for implementation of any sanctions. Cooperation with and among individual states and international organizations is crucial to implementing sanctions that target the DPRK's cyber-related officials and organizations. Also, further integration of norms of state behavior in cyberspace, beyond their affirmation by the UN's Group of Government Experts (GGE), in each state's respective domestic and foreign policies is integral to curbing the DPRK's operational freedom outside its territory.

When the United States establishes a declaratory policy, announces sanctions to implement such policies, and meshes its principles with relevant international norms, the next step would be to start operationalizing such measures by working with allies and partners with an existing shared understanding and cooperative base. Regional and international cooperation through existing working relationships will not only provide a stronger practical basis for implementation, but also would signal a greater resolve and commitment to confronting the issues.

It also may be that the mere process of working with individual states and international organizations on this issue would provide important opportunities for the United States to further lead the larger international conversation on how cyberspace should be governed and managed by the international community. The process of working on tackling a tangible case of malicious cyber activity, rather than a theoretical debate based on hypothetical situations, may help states to come to agreement on a number of issues currently in debate.

Recommendations for the U.S.-ROK Alliance

Cyber cooperation between the United States and ROK has the potential to grow beyond just responding to North Korea's cyber threat into a robust partnership that could serve as a linchpin for advancing both countries' broader cyber interests regionally and globally. The resilience and robustness of the U.S.-ROK alliance is a unique asset for dealing with North Korea's cyber threat. Over the past decades, the two states have developed shared strategic concepts, operational readiness, and a culture of cooperation across multiple sectors. In the current international environment where there are very little shared norms and standards regarding cyberspace, the alliance's development of shared principles and procedures for dealing with cyber attacks may serve as an important precedent and basis for further regional and international norms development.

The two states have started to cooperate on this topic on multiple fronts. Most notably, they established the Cyber Cooperation Working Group after a series of high-profile disruptive cyber attacks against South Korean banks and media agencies in 2013. First meeting in February 2014, the group reportedly discussed defense-related issues such as joint warfare capabilities, intelligence sharing, and training programs, and conducted a tabletop exercise.[20] The bilateral Cyber Policy Consultations is another whole-of-government effort that coordinates on broader cyber policy issues, including international norms, confidence building measures, and Internet governance. In addition to the formal government channels, there is a working relationship between the two national-level computer emergency response teams (CERTs) as well as informal forums in the private sector on the topic of information and communication technology (ICT).

PREPARE A GRADIENT OF RESPONSES

The United States and ROK should develop contingency plans and a menu of corresponding response options for a range of scenarios affected by North Korea's cyber operations. These scenarios should not be necessarily limited exclusively to cyber operations, as North Korea may launch joint provocations in the future. Because cyber operations may be conducted alongside conventional military operations, which the DPRK has already done with electronic warfare capabilities, the United States and ROK should be prepared to react to mixed provocations that will not and should not elicit responses purely in cyber space.

A range of options from declaratory statements to operations aimed at degrading North Korean assets should be assessed. War gaming and continued preparation for future crises will continue to be vital. While the expected intensity of DPRK cyber operations will probably remain relatively low, this level of intensity still includes things similar to the attacks against Sony and the South Korean banking sector. The United States and ROK should be prepared to respond to North Korean attacks of this intensity and higher, essentially being able to dial up a response to the appropriate level of intensity and damage.

---

20. Stephen Noerper, "US-Korea Relations: Strengthened Resolve as North Korea Rumbles," *Comparative Connections* 16, no. 1 (May 2014).

Additionally, contingency plans should be made for a variety of scenarios where cyber operations could play a role. Incidents involving North Korea have a particular tendency to escalate into political and military problems, so the United States and ROK should engage in contingency planning for unexpectedly damaging or intense cyber operations or provocations involving cyber operations.

The scope of contingencies considered should go beyond the Korean peninsula and should incorporate the impact on other regional U.S. allies such as Japan, and other important strategic assets in the region such as early warning networks. The Cyber Cooperation Working Group, as the current key bilateral cyber defense dialogue, remains a good mechanism for further concrete discussions on this topic.

IDENTIFY AND LEVERAGE THE DPRK'S VULNERABILITIES

The U.S.-ROK alliance should consider exploiting North Korea's vulnerability to outside information otherwise restricted by the government. One realistic response option to North Korea's cyber attacks may be to leverage the regime's obsession with tight control on information within the country. One of North Korea's largest asymmetric vulnerabilities is its need to keep a tight control on information within the country. Targeting this asymmetric vulnerability may be an efficient means of changing North Korea's actions. The continuous introduction of information and media digitally into North Korean networks would create pressure that could be utilized, possibly in conjunctions with sanctions or countermeasures, to bring North Korea back into compliance if illicit cyber operations continue.

The DPRK government is known to oppose the consumption of South Korean and foreign media such as news, dramas, music, and the like. Additionally, North Korea has publicly expressed sensitivity to criticism and perceived defamation regarding the character of its leadership and the Kim family in particular. The deliberate introduction of additional media and information into North Korea's networks and population may serve as a potent means of responding to cyber attacks without resorting to uses of force, armed attacks, or countermeasures. The introduction of information and freeing of peoples from censorship falls in line with the U.S. State Department's stated policy goals of increasing Internet freedom for repressed peoples.

While a specific technical policy recommendation is difficult, it should be made a policy goal to introduce some means of free information access or distribution within the North Korean populace, even if that only means reaching elites with computer access. In a similar vein to the United States and ROK being target-rich environments for network attacks, the DPRK is a target-rich environment for information disclosure and transparency measures.

ASSESS EFFECTS ON STRATEGIC BALANCE

The U.S.-ROK alliance should review the possibility that North Korea's growing cyber power may affect the current strategic balance on the Korean peninsula. There should be a broad bilateral strategic assessment, beyond a discussion on joint cyber defense, on how DPRK's growing cyber capabilities affect the larger balance of power on the Korean peninsula. While current discussions on joint cyber defense are critical at the tactical and operational level, the dialogue should expand beyond the purely cyber realm into other important operational environments affected by cyber capabilities.

Following their electronic warfare and irregular operations tradition, North Korea may use cyber capabilities not only as stand-alone provocations but also as a supporting or enabling component for other elements of its military force. This means that North Korea's cyber capabilities can potentially enhance the effectiveness of its operations or degrade the effectiveness of U.S. and ROK defenses.

MITIGATE ALLIANCE VULNERABILITIES

Vulnerabilities in interoperability arising from the current hub-and-spokes alliance structure should be actively mitigated. If North Korea's cyber capabilities are increasingly integrated with its conventional military elements, the U.S.-ROK alliance needs to mitigate its inherent vulnerabilities. Alliance networks, military units, and early warning systems must be interoperable and hardened against disruptive cyber operations. North Korea *is not at this point yet*. However, trends indicate it possibly could move toward targeting military assets. The U.S.-ROK alliance structure should be ready to defend against this capacity.

All spokes in the alliance that are regionally involved, specifically South Korea and Japan, even if not directly allied, must cooperate with each other and the United States to track and protect network-dependent assets, such as early warning systems, against cyber attacks. Cyber units in each country must be capable of efficiently communicating and working together to manage threats that stretch beyond the Korean peninsula. Members of the U.S. alliances in the region should cooperate militarily to ensure that conventional military operations are not impeded by disruptive cyber operations, especially for high-precision operations such as ballistic missile defense and air early warning.

National ballistic missile systems and integrated air defense systems (IADS) are particularly network-dependent technologies relied upon by the United States and ROK. Missile and air threats require fast decisionmaking and the rapid collection and dissemination of telemetry if threats are to be addressed and mitigated. The integration of missile and air defenses with national and allied radar systems both on land and at sea adds depth and strength to the defense network, while also adding numerous points of entry and exploitable vulnerabilities for network intrusion. As the United States and ROK consider deepening missile defense ties and as the North Korean missile program grows in sophistication, it will be increasingly important to maintain a strong cybersecurity regime. Missile defenses are incredibly expensive and complex and North Korea's cyber capabilities could erode or even defeat missile defense systems. This also extends to C4ISR, logistical networks, and weather data, all of which are vital to the functions of a network-centric army and navy.

ENCOURAGE INFORMATION SHARING OUTSIDE OF GOVERNMENT ENTITIES

Information-sharing arrangements, beyond intelligence and government agencies, should be encouraged. The United States should establish a series of robust information-sharing arrangements with individual ROK sectors. Much insight can be gained about North Korea's tactics, techniques, and procedures (TTPs) through examining its past activity against South Korea. Most of North Korea's malicious cyber activity in the past decade has been directed against South Korean military, government, and private entities, and there are many lessons to be learned through examining past attacks or cases of network exploitation to assess how North Korea might target the United States in the future.

The malware used for wiping Sony's hard drives in November 2014 was surprisingly similar to the one used for the March 2013 attacks on South Korean banks. While what North Korea hopes to achieve vis-à-vis the United States may be different and therefore South Korean case studies may not be fully applicable, keeping abreast of security incidents in South Korea may help create a better threat profile of North Korea. If such information is aggregated, disseminated, and acted upon fast enough, it can either help detect malicious activity at the initial exploitation phase and allow the defender enough time to stop an attack, gather information, or perform counterintelligence. In theory, over time this would force North Korea to develop alternative TTPs more often, making offensive cyber operations more costly and cumbersome.

The real challenge is in creating practical information-sharing arrangements that are not only timely and efficient but overcomes any legal or privacy concerns. In theory, there is little disagreement behind the idea that information sharing is one of the most important components of mitigating the strategic disadvantages of cyber defense. In practice, however, there are grave challenges even at the domestic level where private organizations have a disincentive to disclose data breaches due to legal and shareholder liabilities. Extending this to the international level complicates the problem even more. It is probably not practical to look for a comprehensive bilateral information-sharing framework that aggregates from multiple sectors under one agreement.

Instead, the U.S. and ROK governments should promote the establishment of multiple but separate layers of separate information-sharing arrangements hinging on established bilateral agency relationships. For example, the respective intelligence agencies should refine ways to share more cyber threat information among themselves under existing intelligence data sharing agreements, and U.S. and ROK CERTs should separately work on ways to better exchange data in formats that work best with their daily operations. In the private sector, cybersecurity companies in each country can either purchase or exchange each other's threat intelligence data feeds. Relevant changes in domestic legislation may help alleviate private-sector fears about voluntary information sharing, as well as the promotion of new data exchange technologies and formats that render threat data anonymous and easily integrate into daily company operations.

ENGAGE IN REGIONAL CONFIDENCE BUILDING MEASURES AND CAPACITY BUILDING

The United States and ROK should continue to engage in regional confidence building measures (CBMs) and capacity building efforts to create more common ground on cyber issues in the Asia-Pacific region, especially with China. The alliance should assume a leadership role in regional cyber capacity building, equipping states to better deal with malicious cyber activity within their territory. Robust technical international cooperation after a cyber incident is often crucial because cyber attacks often transit through multiple state jurisdictions. The victim state needs cooperation from the transit states to gather further evidence regarding the attack. Furthermore, if a state lacks the capacity to legally prosecute or technically clean up enabling cyber infrastructure, such as botnets within its territory, the transit state can become a safe haven for malicious cyber activity. In Asia, both the United States and ROK have an interest as well as the capacity to enable states to better deal with their domestic cybersecurity problems, providing assistance when requested to do so.

Cyber capacity building should first include helping states to formulate a national cybersecurity strategy that defines the roles and relationships among states' technical and policy apparatus for a cybersecurity objective. This review should be a whole-of-government approach that encompasses the states' foreign, defense, and science ministries as well as national-level CERTs, computer security incident response teams (CSIRTs), and law enforcement agencies. This helps identify gaps in capacity or authority and a rational for investing in closing such gaps. Training and exercise programs focusing on technical incident response capacity and forensic research are also crucial for workforce development.

Several initiatives are already under way in the region, and the U.S.-ROK alliance should leverage existing efforts and assume leadership in areas where possible. The more sophisticated national-level CERTs such as KrCERT and JPCERT frequently host technical training programs individually. APCERT, a collaborative network of national CERTs in the Asia-Pacific, also conducts joint research and training. The Asia-Pacific Economic Cooperation (APEC) Telecommunications and Information Working Group (TEL) has had agreements on promoting regional capacity building. Interpol recently established a center in Singapore for capacity building in cyber crime, and International Telecommunication Union–International Multilateral Partnership Against Cyber Threats (ITU-IMPACT) maintains cybersecurity capacity building assistance programs. Consistent support for these initiatives, coupled with a clear rationale and vision for its necessity, may help the region become much less conducive to malicious cyber activity.

FURTHER ENTRENCH NORMS

The U.S.-ROK alliance should leverage existing bilateral coordination on international norms and standards as a platform for further adoption regionally and globally. The United States and ROK should coordinate closely on developing a common understanding of international norms and standards applicable to cyberspace, and engage in joint efforts to promote their adoption in regional and global forums. North Korea's aggressive behavior in cyberspace has provided additional impetus for the U.S.-ROK alliance to closely consult with each other on delineating the range of aggressive behavior in cyberspace under existing international law and what the appropriate responses would be for each scenario. This has allowed the alliance to coordinate positions on big issues in international cyber norms for application in real situations, from the Law of Armed Conflict (LOAC) applicable to cyberspace to Internet governance. Continued North Korean offensive cyber operations is likely going to push the U.S.-ROK alliance to refine and internalize what are still fuzzy concepts in international law.

Such precedents can be used as an important basis for a joint campaign for its greater adoption in regional forums such as APEC and Association of Southeast Asian Nations (ASEAN) or at global conferences such as UN GGE and ITU meetings. Both governments have an incentive to increase the adoption of such norms internationally, so that more states form similar baseline expectations about state behavior in cyberspace and an agreement regarding culpability and remedies when a cyber attack has occurred.

FINAL NOTES

North Korea is developing and utilizing cyber capabilities in accordance with its asymmetric national and military strategies. The threat of provocative cyber operations launched against the United States and South Korea is increasing and will continue to do so unless certain policy measures are enacted that target North Korea's ability and will to conduct malicious cyber operations.

The DPRK has historically pursued asymmetric advantages over the United States and ROK. The expansion of its cyber capabilities is a logical addition to its commandos, ballistic missiles, and weapons of mass destruction. Cyber capabilities allow the DPRK to mitigate many of the risks associated with other forms of provocation and gain a limited advantage on the Korean peninsula in at least one field. While the DPRK lags in economic and conventional military power, pursuing asymmetric provocative capabilities that it is willing to utilize gives it the ability to erode U.S. and ROK positions while potentially building up its own.

North Korea's cyber capabilities are mainly under control of the RGB, an organization associated with violent provocations, terrorist attacks, and intelligence operations. There is no indication that the RGB is changing any of its missions or goals, and thus there is no reason to assume that its cyber capabilities will be used for exclusively benign purposes or nonprovocative intelligence gathering. The RGB has been repeatedly sanctioned by the international community. Additional smart sanctions or other forms of pressure may be warranted. From the U.S.-ROK perspective, the RGB is a clandestine entity that exists for largely nefarious purposes and should be both monitored and, if possible, additionally exposed in open-source literature to analysts outside of just the United States and ROK intelligence communities.

In the future, North Korea's cyber operations, if unrestrained, are either likely to remain low intensity but be more frequent, or escalate to a more intense form of attack due to misperceptions and miscalculations. They are also more likely to be integrated with other operational elements of North Korea's armed forces.

Policy options are limited when it comes to responding to North Korea's cyber attacks that fall below the use of force threshold. There are some options for a proportional response, such as countermeasures if a breach of sovereignty has occurred as the result of an internationally wrongful act. Beyond a debate on response measures, a broader policy goal should be to curb North Korea's ability and will to launch cyber operations by altering its operational environment. The U.S.-ROK alliance has a good existing framework from which this policy goal can be achieved.

This publication fills a void in current research on North Korea's cyber operations by attempting to bring together previously distinct fields of study, including international relations, military strategy, cybersecurity, and Korea studies. It also brings together English- and Korean-language material as research resources. However, this topic still remains far from elucidated in a comprehensive manner. Deeper research from experts from each respective field is needed. This publication aimed to demystify the topic and spur further research and interest on the topic and increase general knowledge of the issues discussed.

Appendix. Disruptive Cyber Operations Commonly Associated with North Korea

Start Date	Event
July 7, 2009	DDoS on 17 U.S. and ROK public and government websites
July 7, 2010	DDoS on ROK government and private-sector websites
March 4, 2011	DDoS on 40 ROK public, government, military, and private websites, including USFK
April 12, 2011	Nonghyup Bank server disrupted, data erased
March 20, 2013	MBR wiper attack shut down 32,000 computers of banks (Nonghyup Bank, Shinhan Bank, Jeju Bank) and media agencies (YTN, KBS, MBC)
March 25, 2013	*DailyNK*, Free North Korea Radio, Nknet, North Korea Intellectuals Society website disrupted
June 25, 2013	DDoS on 16 government and media websites, targeted DNS servers
November 24, 2014	MBR wiper attack against Sony Pictures Entertainment
December 2014	Data exfiltration, extortion, attempted MBR wiper attack on Korea Hydro & Nuclear Power

Bibliography

Abrahamian, Andray. "North Korea's Unlikely Tech Startups." *Guardian*, September 22, 2014. http://www.theguardian.com/world/2014/sep/22/north-korea-tech-startups.

Abrams, Marshall, and Joe Weiss, "Malicious Control System Cyber Security Attack Case Study–Maroochy Water Services, Australia." Gaithersburg, MD: National Institute of Standards and Technology, 2008. http://csrc.nist.gov/groups/SMA/fisma/ics/documents /Maroochy-Water-Services-Case-Study_report.pdf.

Ahn, Sung-kyu, and Hyo-sik Jung. "Kim Jung-Nam Lead Establishment of KCC, the Core Effort of North Korea's Cyber Warfare." *Joongang Ilbo*, July 12, 2009. http://nk.joins.com /news/view.asp?aid=3418751.

Ahn, Yong-hyun. "North Korea's Electronic Warfare Capability?" *Chosun Ilbo*, March 7, 2011. http://news.chosun.com/site/data/html_dir/2011/03/07/2011030702345.html.

Arquilla, John, and David Ronfeldt. "Cyberwar Is Coming!" Santa Monica, CA: RAND Corporation, 1993. http://www.rand.org/pubs/reprints/RP223.

Bechtol Jr., Bruce E. "Maintaining a Rogue Military: North Korea's Military Capabilities and Strategy at the End of the Kim Jong-Il Era." *International Journal of Korean Studies* 16, no. 1 (2012): 160–191. http://connection.ebscohost.com/c/articles/78327478 /maintaining-rogue-military-north-koreas-military-capabilities-strategy-end-kim -jong-il-era.

Bennett, Bruce W., Christopher P. Twomey, and Gregory F. Treverton. *What Are Asymmetric Strategies?* Santa Monica, CA: RAND Publishing, 1999.

Bermudez Jr., Joseph S. *The Armed Forces of North Korea*. London: I. B. Tauris, 2001.

———. "A New Emphasis on Operations Against South Korea?" 38 North Special Report, U.S. Korea Institute at School of Advanced International Studies (SAIS), 2010. http://38north .org/wp-content/uploads/2010/06/38north_SR_Bermudez2.pdf.

———. *North Korean Special Forces*. Annapolis, MD: Naval Institute Press, 1997.

———. "North Korea's Strategic Culture." Comparative Strategic Cultures Curriculum Project, Science Applications International Corporation (SAIC). Washington, DC: Defense Threat Reduction Agency, October 31, 2006.

Billo, Charles, and Welton Chang. "Cyber Warfare: An Analysis of the Means and Motivations of Selected Nation States." Hanover: Institute of Security Technology Studies at Dartmouth College, 2004.

Bonner III, E. Lincoln. "Cyber Power in 21st-Century Joint Warfare." *Joint Force Quarterly* 74 (2014): 102–109.

Bradner, Eric. "Obama: North Korea's Hack Not War, but 'Cybervandalism.'" CNN, December 24, 2014. http://www.cnn.com/2014/12/21/politics/obama-north-koreas-hack-not-war-but-cyber-vandalism/index.html.

Bumgarner, John, and Scott Borg. *Overview by the US-CCU of the Cyber Campaign against Georgia in August of 2008*. Washington, DC: U.S. Cyber Consequences Unit, 2009. http://www.registan.net/wp-content/uploads/2009/08/US-CCU-Georgia-Cyber-Campaign-Overview.pdf.

Carr, Jeffrey. *Inside Cyber Warfare: Mapping the Cyber Underworld*. Sebastopol: O'Reilly Media, 2011.

Cartwright, James E. "Memorandum for Chiefs of the Military Services Commanders of the Combatant Commands Directors of the Joint Staff Directorates." Joint Chiefs of Staff, November 2010. http://www.nsci-va.org/CyberReferenceLib/2010-11-joint%20Terminology%20for%20Cyberspace%20Operations.pdf.

Cha, Victor D. "Hawk Engagement and Preventive Defense on the Korean Peninsula." *International Security* 27, no. 1 (Summer 2002): 40–78.

Chang, Amy. *Warring State: China's Cybersecurity Strategy*. Washington, DC: Center for New American Security, 2014.

Cho, Seung-ho. "North Korea Has Trained about 3,000 Hackers." *DongA Ilbo*, March 21, 2013. http://news.donga.com/rel/3/all/20130321/53855571/1.

Choi, Bongsik. *The North Korea Industry 2010*. Seoul: Korea Finance Corporation, 2010. http://nkinfo.unikorea.go.kr/nkp/overview/nkOverview.do?sumryMenuId=EC220.

Choi, In-soo. "Jae-Joon Nam, the Head of National Intelligence Service, Opposes Handing over Anti-Communist Investigation but Instead Gives a Detailed Report on North Korea's Cyber Psychological Warfare." *Joongang Ilbo*, November 4, 2013. http://article.joins.com/news/article/article.asp?Total_Id=13047219.

Choi, Sung. "North Korea's IT Application Software Development Center–Pyongyang Information Centre (PIC)." *Korea IT Times*, December 6, 2010. http://www.koreaittimes.com/story/11950/north-korea%E2%80%99s-it-application-software-development-center-pyongyang-information-centre-pi.

Choi, Sunyoung. "North Korea's Sabotage Organizations against South Korea Merged as General Reconnaissance Bureau." *Yonhap News*, May 10, 2009. http://www.yonhapnews.co.kr/politics/2009/05/09/0521000000AKR20090509041100014.HTML.

Chun, Sang-sook. "Rangoon Bombing Incident." National Archives of Korea, December 1, 2006. http://www.archives.go.kr/next/search/listSubjectDescription.do?id=002844 &pageFlag=.

"Civilian-Government-Military Joint Response Team Discloses Interim Investigation Results on the 'March 20 Cyberterror.'" Ministry of Science, ICT, and Future Planning (MSIP), October 2013.

Clapper, James R. "Remarks as Delivered by DNI James R. Clapper on 'National Intelligence, North Korea, and the National Cyber Discussion' at the International Conference on Cyber Security." Fordham University, January 7, 2015. http://www.dni.gov/index.php /newsroom/speeches-and-interviews/208-speeches-interviews-2015/1156-remarks-as -delivered-by-dni-james-r-clapper-on-%E2%80%9Cnational-intelligence,-north-korea, -and-the-national-cyber-discussion%E2%80%9D-at-the-international-conference-on -cyber-security.

Clarke, Richard A., and Robert Knake. *Cyber War: The Next Threat to National Security and What to Do About It*. New York: Ecco, 2011.

Cordesman, Anthony H. *The Korean Military Balance*. Washington, DC: Center for Strategic and International Studies, 2011. http://csis.org/publication/korean-military-balance.

CSIS Korea Chair. *Record of North Korea's Major Conventional Provocations since 1960s*. Center for Strategic and International Studies, 2010. http://csis.org/publication/record -north-koreas-major-conventional-provocations-1960s.

Deeks, Ashley. "Tallinn 2.0 and a Chinese View on the Tallinn Process." *Lawfare*, May 31, 2015. https://www.lawfareblog.com/tallinn-20-and-chinese-view-tallinn-process.

"Democratic People's Republic of Korea." CORI Country Report. Country of Origin Research and Information, 2012. http://www.refworld.org/docid/50ed7d742.html.

Erlendson, Jennifer J. "North Korean Strategic Strategy: Combining Conventional Warfare with the Asymmetrical Effects of Cyber Warfare." Utica College, 2013. http://www.ecii .edu/wp-content/uploads/2013/10/Erlendson-Cohort-4-Draz-North-Korean-Strategic -Strategy-Combining-Conventional-Warfare-with-Asymmetrical-Effects-of-Cyber -Warfare-May-2013.pdf.

FBI, *Update on Sony Investigation*. Washington, DC: FBI National Press Office, 2014. https:// www.fbi.gov/news/pressrel/press-releases/update-on-sony-investigation.

Feakin, Tobias. "Playing Blind-Man's Buff: Estimating North Korea's Cyber Capabilities." *International Journal of Korean Unification Studies* 22, no. 2 (2013).

Follath, Erich, and Holger Stark. "The Story of 'Operation Orchard': How Israel Destroyed Syria's Al Kibar Nuclear Reactor." Spiegel Online, November 2, 2009. http://www.spiegel .de/international/world/the-story-of-operation-orchard-how-israel-destroyed-syria-s-al -kibar-nuclear-reactor-a-658663.html.

Freedman, Lawrence. "The Revolution in Military Affairs." In *Strategy: A History*, 215–236. New York: Oxford University Press, 2013.

Gause, Ken E. *North Korean Civil-Military Trends: Military-First Politics to a Point*. Carlisle, PA: Strategic Studies Institute, 2006. http://www.strategicstudiesinstitute.army.mil /pdffiles/pub728.pdf.

"General Staff Department." North Korea Leadership Watch, January 16, 2011. https:// nkleadershipwatch.wordpress.com/dprk-security-apparatus/general-staff-department/.

"Gen. Kim Yong Chol." North Korea Leadership Watch. Accessed November 18, 2015. https:// nkleadershipwatch.wordpress.com/leadership-biographies/lt-gen-kim-yong-chol/.

Gjelten, Tom. "Pentagon Goes on the Offensive against Cyberattacks." NPR, February 11, 2013. http://www.npr.org/2013/02/11/171677247/pentagon-goes-on-the-offensive-against -cyber-attacks.

GlobalSecurity.org. "Light Infantry Guide Bureau / Reconnaissance Bureau / Special Purpose Forces Command." Accessed November 18, 2015. http://www.globalsecurity.org /military/world/dprk/spf.htm.

———. "Order of Battle—Korean People's Army." Accessed November 18, 2015. http://www .globalsecurity.org/military/world/dprk/kpa-orbat.htm.

Ha, Tae-kyung. *From Leaflets to DDoS Attacks: The Present and the Future of North Korea's Cyber Terror against the South*. Seoul: Geultong, 2013. http://book.naver.com/bookdb /book_detail.nhn?bid=7183692.

Hagen, Andreas. *The Russo-Georgian War of 2008: The Role of the Cyber Attacks in the Conflict*. Fairfax, VA: AFCEA International, 2012. http://www.afcea.org/committees/cyber /documents/TheRusso-GeorgianWar2008.pdf.

Hassig, Kongdan Oh. "North Korean Policy Elites." IDA Paper. Institute for Defense Analyses, n.d. http://www.nkeconwatch.com/nk-uploads/dprkpolicyelites.pdf.

Hathaway, Melissa E. and Alexander Klimburg. "1.2 Cyber Terms and Definitions." In *National Cybersecurity Framework Manual*, edited by Alexander Klimburg. Tallinn, Estonia: NATO CCD COE Publications, 2012.

"The Head of North Korea's General Reconnaissance Bureau Kim Yong-Chol Directly Ordered Sony Hacking." *MK News*, March 8, 2015. http://news.mk.co.kr/newsRead.php ?year=2015&no=220454&utm_source=facebook&utm_medium=sns&utm_campaign =share.

Healey, Jason, and Karl Grindal, eds. *A Fierce Domain: Conflict in Cyberspace, 1986 to 2012*. Vienna, VA: Cyber Conflict Studies Association, 2013.

Hodge, Homer T. "North Korea's Military Strategy." *Strategic Studies Institute Parameters* (2003): 68–81.

Hollis, David. *SWJ Blog. Small Wars Journal*, January 6, 2011. http://smallwarsjournal.com/blog/journal/docs-temp/639-hollis.pdf.

Hong, Sung-bum. "Research on the Current State of North Korea's Science Technology by Area." *Policy Research, Science and Technology Policy Institute* 1, no. 20 (2002). http://www.stepi.re.kr/app/report/view.jsp?cmsCd=CM0012&categCd=A0201&ntNo=270.

HP Security Research. "Profiling an Enigma: The Mystery of North Korea's Cyber Threat Landscape." HP Security Briefing, August 2014. http://h30499.www3.hp.com/t5/HP-Security-Research-Blog/HP-Security-Briefing-episode-16-Profiling-an-enigma-North-Korea/ba-p/6588592.

IHS Jane's Intelligence Review. "Current North Korean Cyber-Warfare Threat to South Korea Would Be Key to Potential War-Fighting Strategy." IHS Jane's 360, January 2015. http://www.janes.com/article/47835/current-north-korean-cyber-warfare-threat-to-south-korea-would-be-key-to-potential-war-fighting-strategy.

Jensen, Eric Talbot. "Cyber Deterrence." *Emory International Law Review* 26 (2012): 773.

Jensen, Rian. "Sovereignty and Neutrality in Cyber Conflict." SSRN Scholarly Paper. Rochester, NY: Social Science Research Network, 2011. http://papers.ssrn.com/abstract=1952598.

———. "State over Society: Science and Technology Policy in North Korea." *USKI Working Paper Series* 9, no. 4 (2009): 1–20. http://uskoreainstitute.org/wp-content/uploads/2010/02/USKI_WP09_Jensen.pdf.

Joo, Sung-ha. "The Fate of the O Kuk Ryol Family." *Pyongyang Story Written in Seoul*, January 29, 2014. http://blog.donga.com/nambukstory/archives/76397.

Jung, Chang-hyun. "Completes Development of an Independent Computer Operating System (OS) from the Perspective of the People's Information Industry." *Minjog21*, December 13, 2012.

Jung, Jae-kwon. "We Have Witnessed the Potential of North Korea's IT Human Resources." *Hankyoreh*, October 29, 2001. http://legacy.www.hani.co.kr/section-003100000/2001/10/003100000200110290350027.html.

Kim, Gui-geun. "North Korea Halts Jamming GPS Signals after 16 Days." *Yonhap News*, May 15, 2012. http://www.yonhapnewstv.co.kr/npost/%eb%b6%81%ed%95%9c-gps-%ea%b5%90%eb%9e%80%ec%a0%84%ed%8c%8c-16%ec%9d%bc-%eb%a7%8c%ec%97%90-%ec%a4%91%eb%8b%a8/.

Kim, Heung-kwang. "Responses and Strategies against North Korea's Cyber Information Warfare." North Korea Intellectuals Solidarity, July 2, 2010. http://www.nkis.kr/board.php?board=nkisb501&page=1&sort=hit&command=body&no=3.

Kim, Hyungsoo. "Kim Jong-Un Says 'Cyber Warfare Is an All-Powerful Tool,' Utilizes It as One of Three Major Means of Warfare." *Joongang Ilbo*, November 5, 2013. http://nk.joins.com/news/view.asp?aid=12640100.

Kim, Jongsun. "Status Quo of North Korea's Software Industry: Focusing on Analysis of the Computer OS, 'Red Star.'" *Korea Exim Bank on North Korea's Economy* (2010): 43–62. http://hope.koreaexim.go.kr/kr/work/check/pub/north_view.jsp?cpage=5&bookNo=706.

"Kim Jong-Un's Instructions from March 8, 2014." North Korea Intellectuals Solidarity, May 29, 2014. http://www.nkis.kr/board.php?board=nkisb201&body_only=y&button_view=n&command=body&no=523.

Kim, Jung-eun. "Kim Jong-Un Takes a Picture with the Members of the Psychological Warfare Unit." *Yonhap News*, November 11, 2013. http://www.yonhapnews.co.kr/politics/2013/11/11/0511000000AKR20131111199400014.HTML.

Kim, Kook-shin. "Summary from Trip to Dandong, China." Korea Institute for National Unification, April 2007.

Kim, Pil-jae. *North Korea's Cyber Invasion of South Korea*. Seoul: Baeknyun Dongahn, 2014. http://www.kyobobook.co.kr/redi_book.jsp?b=9791195263882&g=KOR.

Kim, Seong-wook. "Roh Administration Found to Have Funded Training of North Korea's IT Human Resources Annually." *New Daily*, June 1, 2010. http://www.newdaily.co.kr/news/article.html?no=37882.

Kim, So-hyun. "Kim Visits Army Unit Spying on S. Korea." *Korea Herald*, April 27, 2010. http://www.koreaherald.com/view.php?ud=20100427000663.

———. "'Reconnaissance General Bureau Is Heart of N.K. Terrorism.'" *Korea Herald*, May 26, 2010. http://www.koreaherald.com/view.php?ud=20100526000675.

Kim, So-yul. "North Korea Involved in Cyber Operations in Dandong since 2004." *DailyNK*, July 12, 2009. http://www.dailynk.com/korean/read.php?cataId=nk00100&num=73841.

Kim, Taegyun. "Discussion for North Korea's Development of Capacity-Building." *National Strategy* 20, no. 4 (2014): 5–35. http://www.sejong.org/boad/bd_news/1/egofiledn.php?conf_seq=3&bd_seq=1413&file_seq=2681.

Kim, Young-yun. "Ways to Promote Internet Exchange and Cooperation between South and North Korea." Korea institute for National Unification, May 2004.

"KJI Visits KPA Unit Involved in Hwang Plot." North Korea Leadership Watch, April 28, 2010. https://nkleadershipwatch.wordpress.com/2010/04/28/kji-visits-kpa-unit-involved-in-hwang-plot/.

"Korea Computer Center." http://www.dprksearch.net/bbs/skin/ggambo7002_board/print.php?id=dprklive&no=40.

"KPA General Staff Denies Cyberattack on ROK." North Korea Leadership Watch, April 13, 2013. https://nkleadershipwatch.wordpress.com/2013/04/13/kpa-general-staff-denies-cyberattack-on-rok/.

Krekel, Bryan, Patton Adams, and George Bakos. *Occupying the Information High Ground: Chinese Capabilities for Computer Network Operations and Cyber Espionage.* Washington, DC: Northrop Grumman Corp, 2012. http://nsarchive.gwu.edu/NSAEBB/NSAEBB424 /docs/Cyber-066.pdf.

Kuehl, Daniel T. "Chapter 2: From Cyberspace to Cyberpower: Defining the Problem." In *Cyberpower and National Security*, edited by Franklin D. Kramer, Stuart H. Starr, and Larry K. Wentz. Washington, DC: National Defense University, 2009.

Kwon, Yang-ju. *The Comprehension of North Korean Military.* Seoul: Korea Institute of Defense Analyses, 2010.

Lee, Bumjin. "If North Korea Was behind Cheonan Sinking, General Reconnaissance Bureau's Kim Yong-Chol Likely to Have Led the Operation . . . Kim Kyuk-Sik of the Fourth Corps Also Plausible." *Chosun Weekly*, May 3, 2010. http://weekly.chosun.com/client /news/viw.asp?ctcd=C01&nNewsNumb=002103100000.

Lee, Chungeun. "Analysis on North Korea's Level of Science Technology and Fields of Interest." Ministry of Unification, December 2009.

Lee, Chungeun, Jong-sun Kim, and Dali Nam. "Policies to Promote South-North ICT Cooperation." Policy Research. Science and Technology Policy Institute, 2014. http://www.stepi .re.kr/app/report/view.jsp?cmsCd=CM0012&categCd=A0201&ntNo=813.

Lee, Hong-yul. "How North Korea Trains Its IT Resources." *Telecommunications Technology Association Journal*, no. 122 (March 2009): 85–91.

Lee, Hwa-jong. "North Korea's Reconnaissance General Bureau's Cyber Unit Match CIA's Capabilities." *Munhwa Ilbo*, March 21, 2013. http://www.etimes.net/Service/CreditBank _2008/ShellView.asp?ArticleID=2013032113540601558.

Lee, Jung-hoon. "Kyung-Hak Jung, the First North Korean Spy Caught during the Roh Administration." *New DongA*, October 1, 2006. http://shindonga.donga.com/docs/magazine /shin/2006/10/13/200610130500016/200610130500016_1.html.

Lee, Kyo-kwan. "The Secret of Korea Computer Center." *NK Chosun*, May 11, 2001. http://nk .chosun.com/news/articleView.html?idxno=6764.

Lee, Michael. "North Korea's Intelligence Operations against South Korea." Chogabje.com, November 3, 2014. http://www.chogabje.com/board/column/view.asp?C_IDX=58208&C _CC=BC.

Lee, Sanghee. "Thoughts on an 'Initiative Strategy' for the Comprehensive Management of North Korea." Brookings Institution, 2010. http://www.brookings.edu/research/papers /2010/04/north-korea-lee.

Lee, Sang-yong. "Members of the Enemy Collapse Bureau, Who Infiltrates South Korea on Backpacks, Meets Kim Jong-Un." *DailyNK*, November 12, 2013. http://www.dailynk.com /korean/read.php?cataId=nk00700&num=101611.

Lee, Seok, and Sang-ki Kim. "Report on Travels from China (Shenyang and Dandong)." Korea Development Institute, 2008. https://www.kdi.re.kr/data/download/attach/12241_28.pdf.

Lee, Seunghyun. "Despite Many Talks, HanaBiz the Only Outcome from Economic Cooperation between North and South Korea." *Tongil News*, March 24, 2004. http://www.tongilnews.com/news/articleView.html?idxno=42717.

Lee, Soo-kyung. "HanaBiz Establishes Hana Program Center, a Joint-Venture between North and South Korea in China, and Initiates Training on Information and Communication." Radio Free Asia, September 13, 2002. http://www.rfa.org/korean/in_focus/89456-20020913.html.

Lee, Soon-hyuk. "Anonymous Says 'Will Launch Cyberattack against North Korea on June 25.'" *Hankyoreh*, May 8, 2013. http://www.hani.co.kr/arti/economy/it/586466.html.

Lee, Suk-woo. "Office 39's New Source of Revenue: Selling Hacking Programs Used in South Korean Game 'Lineage.'" *Chosun Ilbo*, August 5, 2011. http://news.chosun.com/site/data/html_dir/2011/08/05/2011080500076.html.

Lee, Young-jong. "Cyber Warfare Is KPA's 'Ruthless Sword.'" *Joongang Ilbo*, December 30, 2014. http://www.sisapress.com/news/articleView.html?idxno=63782.

Lewis, James A. "Cyber Cooperation in Northeast Asia," *NBR*, March 17, 2015. http://www.nbr.org/research/activity.aspx?id=541.

Lewis, James A., and Katrina Timlin. "Cybersecurity and Cyberwarfare: Preliminary Assessment of National Doctrine and Organization." United Nations Institute for Disarmament Research, October 2011.

Lim, Jong-in. "Major Countries around the World Are Preparing for Cyber Warfare Aggressively." *Science and Technology* 528, no. 5 (2013). http://www.kofst.or.kr/kofst/PDF/2013/n5s528/GGDCBE_2013_n5s528_52.pdf.

Mansourov, Alexandre Y., ed. *Bytes and Bullets: Information Technology Revolution and National Security on the Korean Peninsula*. Honolulu, HI: Asia-Pacific Center for Security Studies, 2005.

———. "North Korea on the Cusp of Digital Transformation." *The Nautilus Institute*, Nautilus Institute Special Report, October 20, 2011. http://www.nautilus.org/wp-content/uploads/2011/12/DPRK_Digital_Transformation.pdf.

———. "North Korea's Cyber Warfare and Challenges for the U.S.-ROK Alliance." KEI Academic Paper Series, Korea Economic Institute of America, 2014. http://keia.org/sites/default/files/publications/kei_aps_mansourov_final.pdf.

McCaney, Kevin. "Army Proposes New Classification for Cyber Warriors." *Defense Systems*, September 5, 2014. https://defensesystems.com/articles/2014/09/05/army-cyber-warrior-new-classification.aspx.

Melvin, Curtis. "KPA Reconnaissance Bureau (Unit 586) Located." North Korean Economy Watch, April 28, 2010. http://www.nkeconwatch.com/2010/04/28/kpa-reconnaissance-bureau-located/.

———. "Pyongyang Information Center (PIC)." North Korean Economy Watch, December 6, 2010. http://www.nkeconwatch.com/category/dprk-organizations/state-offices/pyongyang-international-information-center-of-new-technology-and-economy/.

Mercado, Stephen C. "Hermit Surfers of P'yongyang." *CIA Studies in Intelligence* 48, no. 1 (2004). https://www.cia.gov/library/center-for-the-study-of-intelligence/csi-publications/csi-studies/studies/vol48no1/article04.html.

Min, Gyung-rak. "Director of the Artillery Bureau of the General Staff, Who Played a Leading Role in the YP-Do Incident, Gets Promoted to General." *Yonhap News*, January 7, 2015. http://www.yonhapnews.co.kr/.

Minnich, James M. *The North Korean People's Army: Origins and Current Tactics.* Annapolis, MD: U.S. Naval Institute Press, 2005.

"Mirim College: Establishment and Current Activity." *NK Chosun*, October 31, 2013. http://nk.chosun.com/bbs/list.html?table=bbs_29&idxno=4282&page=2&total=112&sc_area=&sc_word=.

Mosendz, Polly. "Hackers Compromise Database of South Koreans Who Work for the U.S. Military." *Wire*, June 5, 2014. http://www.thewire.com/technology/2014/06/database-of-south-koreans-working-for-us-military-hacked/372225/.

Murauskaite, Egle. "North Korea's Cyber Capabilities: Deterrence and Stability in a Changing Strategic Environment." *38 North*, September 12, 2014. http://38north.org/2014/09/emurauskaite091214/.

Namgoong, Min. "North Korea's Reconnaissance Bureau Is a Direct Subordinate Organization under the National Defence Commission." *DailyNK*, April 21, 2010. http://www.dailynk.com/korean/read.php?cataId=nk01500&num=82869.

"National Numbering Plan of the DPRK." International Telecommunication Union, 2011. https://www.itu.int/dms_pub/itu-t/oth/02/02/T02020000360001MSWE.docx.

"Nerve Center of DPRK's Anti-ROK Operations." North Korea Leadership Watch, May 27, 2010. https://nkleadershipwatch.wordpress.com/2010/05/27/nerve-center-of-dprks-anti-rok-operations/.

"NIS Head Nam Jae-Joon Says 'Cannot Transfer Authority to Investigate Anti-Communism Efforts' . . . Reports Extensively on North Korean Cyber Psychological Warfare." *Joongang Ilbo*, November 4, 2013. http://article.joins.com/news/article/article.asp?Total_Id=13047219.

"N. Korea Still Jamming GPS Signals." *Chosun Ilbo*, March 10, 2011. http://english.chosun.com/site/data/html_dir/2011/03/10/2011031000575.html.

Noerper, Stephen. "US-Korea Relations: Strengthened Resolve as North Korea Rumbles," *Comparative Connections* 16, no. 1 (May 2014).

"North Korea Elevates Its Korea Computer Center's Status to Ministerial Level," *NK Chosun*, February 21, 2001, http://nk.chosun.com/news/articleView.html?idxno=4301.

"North Korea Employs All of Its Cyber Units Including Bureau 121 to Hack Information on Warhead Miniaturization and Ballistic Missile Technology." North Korea Intellectuals Solidarity, November 5, 2014. http://www.nkis.kr/board.php?board=nkisb201 &command=body&no=553.

"North Korea Newly Establishes Game Sabotage Unit in General Reconnaissance Bureau's Bureau 121, Deployed to Gather Foreign Currency." North Korea Intellectuals Solidarity, August 8, 2013. http://www.nkis.kr/board.php?board=nkisb201&command=body&no =533.

"North Korea's Electronic/Cyber Warfare Capabilities (Questionnaires from the Ministry of National Defense)." *News Can*, September 25, 2005. http://www.newscani.com/news /articleView.html?idxno=3375.

"North Korea's Electronic Warfare Capabilities." *Nkpark's Blog*. https://nkpark.wordpress .com/2011/03/08/%eb%b6%81%ed%95%9c-%ec%a0%84%ec%9e%90%ec%a0%84 -%eb%8a%a5%eb%a0%a5%ec%9d%80/.

"North Korea's Hacking Unit Elevated from Battalion to Brigade-Level through Reinforce-ment." North Korea Intellectuals Solidarity, August 8, 2013. http://www.nkis.kr/board .php?board=nkisb201&page=5&command=body&no=472.

"North Korea's Internal State of Affairs." *Korea Institute for National Unification Monthly North Korea Review* 3, no. 4 (2009): 14–21. http://www.kinu.or.kr/report/report_02_01.jsp ?page=4&num=169&mode=view&field=&text=&order=&dir=&bid=DATA03&ses= &category=13.

"North Korea's Korea Computer Center (KCC)." *Internet and Security*, March 21, 2012. http:// viruslab.tistory.com/2523.

"North Korea's Korea Computer Center Status Elevated to Ministerial Level." *NK Chosun*, February 21, 2001. http://nk.chosun.com/news/articleView.html?idxno=4301.

"North Korea's Power Structure." Ministry of Unification, Institute for Unification Educa-tion, n.d. https://cloud.uniedu.go.kr/uniedu/home/pds/pdsatcl/view.do?id=1549&mid =SM00000170.

Oh, Myung-ho, Myung-hwan Park, and Jae-ryong Hwang. *Intro to Cyber Warfare*. Seoul: Yangseogak, 2013. http://book.naver.com/bookdb/book_detail.nhn?bid=7438065.

Oh, Seok-min. "N. Korea Boosts Cyber Operations Capabilities." Yonhap News Agency, May 10, 2015. http://english.yonhapnews.co.kr/news/2015/05/08/97/0200000000 AEN20150508006900315F.html.

Park, Chan-mo. "New Prospects in Science Technology Cooperation between North and South Korea." Presentation at Forum on Science Technology Policy hosted by Science and Technology Policy Institute, Seoul, South Korea, 2012. http://www.stepi.re.kr/module/forumDownFile.jsp?cmsCd=CM0037&ntNo=14999&sbNo=1&fileFlag=spk.

Park, Geun-tae. "Information on Pyongyang University of Science Technology, Where Google CEO Has Recently Made a Visit." *ChosunBiz*, January 9, 2013. http://biz.chosun.com/site/data/html_dir/2013/01/09/2013010902018.html.

Park, Jong-duk. "North Korea Ranks 3rd in Cyber Power, Maintains a 30,000 Cyber Army." *Daily Journal*, August 13, 2013. http://www.dailyjn.com/news/articleView.html?idxno=14568.

Park, Soonpyo. "North Korea Responsible for Most of 70,000 Cases of Cyberattacks during the Last Five Years." YTN, March 21, 2013. http://www.ytn.co.kr/_ln/0101_201303211024217337?ems=12714.

Park, Sung-kook. "Tasks of the General Bureau of Reconnaissance." *DailyNK*, May 7, 2010. http://www.dailynk.com//english/read.php?cataId=nk02900&num=6341.

Paul, Christopher, Isaac R. Porche, and Elliot Axelband. "The Other Quiet Professionals: Lessons for Future Cyber Forces from the Evolution of Special Forces." Santa Monica, CA: RAND Corporation, 2014. http://www.rand.org/pubs/research_reports/RR780.

"Periodical Engine Update–April 9, 2003." V3 MSS AhnLab, April 9, 2003. http://v3mss.ahnlab.com/front/board/update_view.do?nowPage=363&board.num=139381.

"Pyongyang Informatics Center." *Digital North Korea Encyclopedia*. https://web.archive.org/web/20150505204551/http://www.kplibrary.com/nkterm/read.aspx?num=989.

Qiao, Liang, and Xiangsui Wang. *Unrestricted Warfare*. Beijing: PLA Literature and Arts Publishing House, 1999.

Rattray, Gregory J. *Strategic Warfare in Cyberspace*. Boston, MA: MIT Press, 2001.

Reed, Thomas C. *At the Abyss: An Insider's History of the Cold War*. New York: Presidio Press, 2005.

Rid, Thomas. *Cyber War Will Not Take Place*. London: Oxford University Press, 2013.

ROK Ministry of Foreign Affairs. "2nd ROK-EU Cyber Policy Consultations to Take Place." April 28, 2015. http://www.mofa.go.kr/webmodule/htsboard/template/read/engreadboard.jsp?typeID=12&boardid=302&seqno=315184.

ROK Ministry of National Defense. *2004 Defense White Paper*. Seoul, South Korea, 2004.

———. *2006 Defense White Paper*. Seoul, South Korea, 2006.

———. *2008 Defense White Paper*. Seoul, South Korea, 2008.

———. *2010 Defense White Paper*. Seoul, South Korea, 2010.

———. *2012 Defense White Paper.* Seoul, South Korea, 2012.

———. *2014 Defense White Paper.* Seoul, South Korea, 2014.

———. *Status on the Analysis of North Korea's Information Warfare Capability.* Seoul, South Korea, 2008. http://bemil.chosun.com/nbrd/bbs/php/downcnt.php?b_bbs_id=10081 &num=79&pn=0&filename=%BA%CF%C7%D1%20%C1%A4%BA%B8%C0%FC%B7% C2%C0%C7%20%B4%C9%B7%C2%20%BA%D0%BC%AE%20%C7%F6%C8%B2.hwp&file _nam=%BA%CF%C7%D1%20%C1%A4%BA%B8%C0%FC%B7%C2%C0%C7%20 %B4%C9%B7%C2%20%BA%D0%BC%AE%20%C7%F6%C8%B2.hwp&postdat=2006-11 -02%2009:57:56&fileidx=489775.

ROK Ministry of Unification. "North Korea Encyclopedia: 5-Year Science Technology Development Plan." North Korea Information Portal. Accessed November 17, 2015. http:// nkinfo.unikorea.go.kr/nkp/term/viewNkKnwldgDicary.do?pageIndex=2&koreanChrctr =&dicaryId=8.

———. "North Korea Encyclopedia: Kim Il-sung Military University." Institute for Unification Education, August 20, 2014. http://www-uniedu-go-kr.nciashield.org/uniedu/etc /nkKnowldgDictionary/view.do?mcd=MC00000633&currPage=3&listScale=20 &pageScale=10&nkKnowledgeDictSn=38.

———. "Profile: Kim Yong-chol." North Korea Information Portal. Accessed November 17, 2015. http://nkinfo.unikorea.go.kr/nkp/theme/viewPeople.do?nkpmno=945.

———. "Profile: O Kuk-ryol." North Korea Information Portal. Accessed November 17, 2015. http://nkinfo.unikorea.go.kr/nkp/theme/viewPeople.do?nkpmno=1072.

Ryu, Hyun-jeong. "Analysis of North Korea's Hacking Capabilities: Has 15-Year Cyber Combat Experience . . . Can Deal a Bigger Blow than Conventional Weapons." *Chosun-Biz*, January 5, 2015. http://biz.chosun.com/site/data/html_dir/2015/01/05/2015010502512 .html.

"Saenuri Party's Testifier Says 'North Korea's Cyber Agents Mess around in South Korean Online Communities.'" JTBC. August 19, 2013. http://news.jtbc.joins.com/article/article .aspx?news_id=NB10328087.

Sanger, David E. "Obama Order Sped Up Wave of Cyberattacks against Iran," *New York Times*, June 1, 2012, http://www.nytimes.com/2012/06/01/world/middleeast/obama -ordered-wave-of-cyberattacks-against-iran.html?_r=0.

Sang-joo Park. "Current Status and Prospects for Opening of North Korea's Internet." *KIDSI Information Communication Policy* 20, no. 15 (2008): 69–72. https://www.kisdi.re.kr/kisdi /fp/kr/publication/selectResearch.do?cmd=fpSelectResearch&sMenuType=2&controlNo =11072&langdiv=1.

Schmitt, Michael N. "In Defense of Due Diligence in Cyberspace." *Yale Law Journal* 125, no. F. 68 (2015). http://www.yalelawjournal.org/forum/in-defense-of-due-diligence-in-cyberspace.

———. "International Law and Cyber Attacks: Sony v. North Korea." Just Security, December 17, 2014. https://www.justsecurity.org/18460/international-humanitarian-law-cyber-attacks-sony-v-north-korea/.

———, ed. *Tallinn Manual on the International Law Applicable to Cyber Warfare*. Cambridge: Cambridge University Press, 2013. http://ebooks.cambridge.org/ref/id/CBO9781139169288.

"The Second in Command within the North Korean Military Is the Director of the KPA General Political Bureau." *Tongil News*, May 3, 2014. http://www.tongilnews.com/news/quickViewArticleView.html?idxno=107136.

Seo, Hyun-jin. "Terms of Agreements on 'Hana Program Center,' the First IT Joint-Venture between North and South Korea." *Minjog21*, May 1, 2001. http://www.minjog21.com/news/quickViewArticleView.html?idxno=597.

Seo, Yoosuk. "Changes in North Korea's Military Policy and Strategy, and Prospects Regarding Tensions in the Yellow Sea." Ministry of Unification, November 2010.

Shin, Choong-geun, and Sang-jin Lee. "A Study of Countermeasure and Strategic Analysis on North Korean Cyber Terror." *Korean National Police University Police Studies Research* 13, no. 4 (2013): 202–225.

Shin, Joon-sik. "Information Regarding Jo Myung-Lae, Person in Charge of North Korea's Hacker Unit." *New Daily*, July 10, 2012. http://www.newdaily.co.kr/news/article.html?no=117038.

Shin, Kwang-young, and Hoon-sang Park. "The North Korean Hacker Who Targeted Online Games Turned out to Be Part of an Organization Subordinate to Office 39." *DongA Ilbo*, August 5, 2011. http://news.donga.com/Politics/3/00/20110805/39319810/1.

Shin, Suk-ho, and Sung-woon Yoo. "South Korea's Military Helpless Fighting Electronic Warfare." *DongA Ilbo*, December 3, 2010. http://news.donga.com/BestClick/3/all/20101203/33035628/1.

Shircliffe, James E. "Information Strategy and Warfare: A Guide to Theory and Practice." *U.S. Army Military Review* 89, no. 4 (2009): 128. http://connection.ebscohost.com/c/book-reviews/43251498/information-strategy-warfare-guide-theory-practice.

Sin, Steve. "Cyber Threat Posed by North Korea and China to South Korea and US Forces Korea." *Defense and Technology* 364 (2009): 28–33.

"South Korea Identified Who's behind the Cyber Attack." IssueMakersLab, April 10, 2013. http://issuemakerslab.com/320/1mission.html.

"South Korea Loses to North Korea in Electronic Warfare . . . Radars Became Dysfunctional from North Korea's EMP Attack." *Newsis*, December 3, 2010. http://www.newsis.com/ar_detail/view.html?ar_id=NISX20101203_0006865372&cID=10211&pID=10200.

"Special Investigative Committee Formed under National Defense Commission." North Korea Leadership Watch, July 4, 2014. https://nkleadershipwatch.wordpress.com/2014/07/04/special-investigative-committee-formed-under-national-defense-commission/.

Suh, Chang-nyong. "North Korea via the Internet." iNews24, October 15, 2003. http://opinion.inews24.com/php/view_print.php?g_serial=100874&g_menu=041700&pay_news=0&access.

Symantec Security Response. "Four Years of DarkSeoul Cyberattacks Against South Korea Continue on Anniversary of Korean War." Symantec Official Blog, June 26, 2013. http://www.symantec.com/connect/blogs/four-years-darkseoul-cyberattacks-against-south-korea-continue-anniversary-korean-war.

Tarakanov, Dmitry. "The 'Kimsuky' Operation: A North Korean APT?" SecureList, September 11, 2013. https://securelist.com/analysis/publications/57915/the-kimsuky-operation-a-north-korean-apt/.

Thayer, Nate. "American Spy Chief Secret Meeting with Head of North Korean Cyber Warfare." Nate Thayer–Journalist, January 9, 2015. http://www.nate-thayer.com/american-spy-chief-secret-meeting-with-head-of-north-korean-cyber-warfare/.

"Understanding North Korea." Seoul: Education Center for Unification, 2014. http://www.unikorea.go.kr/content.do?cmsid=1762&mode=view&page=&cid=41603.

United Nations. *UN Legislative Series: Materials on the Responsibility of States for Internationally Wrongful Acts*. New York, 2012. http://legal.un.org/legislativeseries/documents/Book25/Book25.pdf.

United Nations General Assembly. *Group of Governmental Experts on Developments in the Field of Information and Telecommunications in the Context of International Security*. New York, 2013. http://www.un.org/ga/search/view_doc.asp?symbol=A/68/98.

———. *Group of Governmental Experts on Developments in the Field of Information and Telecommunications in the Context of International Security*. New York, 2015. http://www.un.org/ga/search/view_doc.asp?symbol=A/70/174.

United Nations Office for Disarmament Affairs. "2015—A/70/172: The Republic of Korea." *GGE Information Security*, July 2015. https://unoda-web.s3.amazonaws.com/wp-content/uploads/2015/08/ROKISinfull.pdf.

———. "Developments in the Field of Information and Telecommunications in the Context of International Security." *GGE Information Security*, July 2015. http://www.un.org/disarmament/topics/informationsecurity/.

———. "Fact Sheet—Developments in the Field of Information and Telecommunications in the Context of International Security." *GGE Information Security*, July 2015. https://unoda-web.s3.amazonaws.com/wp-content/uploads/2015/07/Information-Security-Fact-Sheet-July2015.pdf.

United Nations Security Council. "Security Council Committee Determines Entities, Goods Subject to Measures Imposed on Democratic People's Republic of Korea by Resolution 1718 (2006)." UN Press Release, May 2012. http://www.un.org/press/en/2012/sc10633.doc.htm.

U.S. Department of Defense. *Joint Communiqué: The 45th ROK-U.S. Security Consultative Meeting.* Washington, DC, 2013. http://www.defense.gov/Portals/1/Documents/pubs/Joint%20Communique_%2045th%20ROK-U.S.%20Security%20Consultative%20Meeting.pdf.

———. *Military and Security Developments Involving the Democratic People's Republic of Korea 2013.* Washington, DC, 2013. http://www.defense.gov/pubs/North_Korea_Military_Power_Report_2013-2014.pdf.

U.S. Department of Justice. *U.S. Charges Five Chinese Military Hackers for Cyber Espionage Against U.S. Corporations and a Labor Organization for Commercial Advantage.* Washington, DC, 2014. http://www.justice.gov/opa/pr/us-charges-five-chinese-military-hackers-cyber-espionage-against-us-corporations-and-labor.

U.S. Department of State. *Joint Statement of the 2014 United States–Republic of Korea Foreign and Defense Ministers' Meeting.* Washington, DC, 2014. http://www.state.gov/r/pa/prs/ps/2014/10/233340.htm.

———. *Joint Statement on United States-Republic of Korea Bilateral Cyber Policy Consultations.* Washington, DC, 2014. http://www.state.gov/r/pa/prs/ps/2014/230869.htm.

U.S. House Science and Technology Committee. *Untangling Attribution: Moving to Accountability in Cyberspace.* 111th Cong., 2nd sess. July 15, 2010.

U.S. President. Executive Order. "Blocking the Property of Certain Persons Engaging in Significant Malicious Cyber-Enabled Activities." *Federal Register* 80, no. 18077 (April 2, 2015): 13694. https://www.federalregister.gov/articles/2015/04/02/2015-07788/blocking-the-property-of-certain-persons-engaging-in-significant-malicious-cyber-enabled-activities.

———. "Imposing Additional Sanctions with Respect to North Korea." *Federal Register* 80, no. 817 (January 6, 2015): 13687. https://www.federalregister.gov/articles/2015/01/06/2015-00058/imposing-additional-sanctions-with-respect-to-north-korea.

U.S. Senate Armed Services Committee. *Inquiry into Cyber Intrusions Affecting U.S. Transportation Command Contractors.* Washington, DC: GPO, 2014.

U.S. Senate Homeland Security and Governmental Affairs Committee. *North Korea: Illicit Activity Funding the Regime.* 109th Cong., 2nd sess., April 25, 2006.

"Virus Profile: W32/Kuang.gen!1BB55FA83B30." McAfee, March 19, 2013. http://home.mcafee.com/virusinfo/virusprofile.aspx?key=2351728#none.

"W32.Weird Technical Details." Symantec, February 13, 2007. http://www.symantec.com/security_response/writeup.jsp?docid=2000-121515-2958-99&tabid=2.

Wallensteen, Peter. *A Century of Economic Sanctions: A Field Revisited*. Uppsala: Uppsala University, 2000.

Wang, Baocun, and Fei Li. "Information Warfare." *Federation of American Scientists: Chinese Intelligence-Related Documents*, June 1995. http://fas.org/irp/world/china/docs/iw _wang.htm.

Wang, Pufeng. "The Challenge of Information Warfare." *Federation of American Scientists: Chinese Intelligence-Related Documents*, 1995. http://fas.org/irp/world/china/docs/iw_mg _wang.htm.

Wei, Jincheng. "Information War: A New Form of People's War." *Federation of American Scientists: Chinese Intelligence-Related Documents*, June 1996. http://fas.org/irp/world /china/docs/iw_wei.htm.

"What Is Pyongyang Informatics Center Like?" *ET News*, February 12, 2001. http://www .etnews.com/200102110005?SNS=00002.

Williams, Martyn. "North Korea's Chinese IP Addresses." North Korea Tech, June 26, 2011. http://www.northkoreatech.org/2011/06/26/north-koreas-chinese-ip-addresses/.

Worden, Robert L. *North Korea: A Country Study*. U.S. Library of Congress Federal Research Division. Washington, DC: GPO, 2008. http://archive.org/details/northkoreacountr 00word.

Yang, Nak-gyu. "Electronic Warfare Tactics as Described in North Korea's Field Manual." *Asia Economy*, April 18, 2011. http://m.asiae.co.kr/view.htm?no=201103070943282 4411#cb.

Yoo, Dong-ryul. *Cyberspace and National Security*. Seoul: Korean Institute of Liberal Democracy, 2012.

Yoo, Kwan-hee. "The Truth about North Korea's 'Storm Corps,' in Charge of Creating Disturbance behind the Scenes during Wartime." *DailyNK*, March 26, 2009. http://www .dailynk.com/korean/read.php?cataId=nk04500&num=69150.

Yoo, Yong-won. "North Korea Imports Equipment That Allows Disruption of the Entire Korean Peninsula." *Chosun Ilbo*, March 7, 2011. http://news.chosun.com/site/data/html _dir/2011/03/07/2011030700169.html.

Zetter, Kim. *Countdown to Zero Day: Stuxnet and the Launch of the World's First Digital Weapon*. New York: Crown, 2014.

About the Project Directors and Authors

Victor D. Cha is a senior adviser and the inaugural holder of the Korea Chair at CSIS. He is also director of Asian studies and holds the D. S. Song–KF Chair in the Department of Government and School of Foreign Service at Georgetown University. From 2004 to 2007, he served as director for Asian affairs at the White House on the National Security Council (NSC), where he was responsible primarily for Japan, the Korean peninsula, Australia/New Zealand, and Pacific Island nation affairs. Dr. Cha was also the deputy head of delegation for the United States at the Six-Party Talks in Beijing and received two Outstanding Service Commendations during his tenure at the NSC. He is the author of *Nuclear North Korea: A Debate on Engagement Strategies*, with Dave Kang (Columbia University Press, 2004); *Beyond the Final Score: The Politics of Sport in Asia* (Columbia University Press, 2009); and *The Impossible State: North Korea, Past and Future* (Ecco, 2012), selected by *Foreign Affairs* as a 2012 "Best Book on Asia and the Pacific." His next book is *Powerplay: Origins of the American Alliance System in Asia* (Princeton University Press, forthcoming). Dr. Cha holds a BA, an MIA, and a PhD from Columbia University, as well as an MA from Oxford University.

James A. Lewis is a senior fellow and director of the Strategic Technologies Program at CSIS. Before joining CSIS, he worked at the Departments of State and Commerce as a Foreign Service officer and as a member of the Senior Executive Service. His government experience includes work on Asian politico-military issues, conventional arms and technology transfers, and military and intelligence-related technologies. Dr. Lewis led the U.S. delegation to the Wassenaar Arrangement Experts Group on advanced civil and military technologies and was the rapporteur for the UN Group of Government Experts on Information Security for their successful 2010 and 2013 sessions. He was assigned to U.S. Southern Command for Operation Just Cause, U.S. Central Command for Operation Desert Shield, and to the U.S. Central American Task Force. Since joining CSIS, Dr. Lewis has authored numerous publications, including *Space Exploration in a Changing International Environment* (CSIS, 2014), *Conflict and Negotiation in Cyberspace* (CSIS, 2013), and *Securing Cyberspace for the 44th Presidency* (CSIS, 2008), which was commended by President Barack Obama. He is an internationally recognized expert, and his comments appear frequently in the media. His current research examines sovereignty on the Internet, cybersecurity norms, warfare, and technological innovation. Dr. Lewis received his PhD from the University of Chicago.

Jenny Jun is an analyst with a research focus on cyber warfare, asymmetric strategies, and security issues in East Asia. She is currently researching the role of information in modern warfare as it relates to military decision cycles. Prior to her graduate studies, she was a cybersecurity consultant at Delta Risk LLC. She is a MA candidate at Georgetown University's Security Studies Program (SSP) and graduated magna cum laude from Georgetown University School of Foreign Service with a certificate in Asian studies. Ms. Jun has published articles on North Korea security issues in the *CSIS Korea Chair Platform*, *38 North*, and *Yonsei Journal of International Studies*. She serves as president of the Sejong Society, a young professional organization affiliated with the U.S.-Korea Institute at Johns Hopkins School of Advanced International Studies.

Scott LaFoy is an analyst focusing on Chinese and North Korean national strategy, military strategy, and asymmetric military capabilities, including cyber, nuclear weapons, and ballistic missile technologies. His other research areas include food security, logistics, satellite imagery analysis, and the Mongolian mining industry. He is the coeditor *Rice & Iron*, a blog addressing food and energy security issues in North Korea, and he is building a wiki-style database for open-source primary documents, intelligence analyses, and satellite imagery signatures. Mr. LaFoy is currently a MA candidate at the Georgetown University Security Studies Program and graduated from Georgetown University with a degree in government.

Ethan Sohn is an analyst whose interests span security dynamics in East Asia to the U.S. energy industry. His research has focused on China-India-Japan relations, and he has participated in the Citizens' Alliance for North Korean Human Rights. Previously, he has served as an army interpreter with the UN Command Security Battalion at the Joint Security Area, Panmunjom. Mr. Sohn graduated from the Georgetown University School of Foreign Service, majoring in international political economy, with a certificate in Asian studies. He is currently a power markets analyst at Pace Global, a Siemens Business.